THE PROCESS

Susan Cambridge, LCSW

The Process

Copyright © 2013 by Susan Cambridge.

Book cover design by Exodus Design Studios (www.exodusdesign.com)

Editing and page design by ChristianEditingServices.com

All the events shared in this book are true, based on Susan Cambridge's own recollections of what occurred at that time. Names, descriptions of people, and some places have been changed to protect the identity and privacy of individuals.

I would like to dedicate this book to my wonderful mother, Dorrett Cambridge. Mom, thank you for being a great inspiration and role model in my life.

Also, I would like to dedicate this book in memory of the one who walked me through my own personal process of healing, deliverance, and restoration—Minister Pamela Parker. The journey has been well worth it.

⌒ Table of Contents ⌒

☞ Acknowledgements ☜

$\mathcal{F}$irst and foremost, I want to thank my Lord and Savior, Jesus Christ, for trusting, equipping, and anointing me to write this powerful book. This is a God-sized dream come true for me. As a young teenager, I hopped on the bus and headed to our local Bible bookstore to shop every week. I was captivated by all the books and always said, "I'm going to write a book one day and have a personal library in my home." Well, seventeen years later, I have written my first book and have a personal library in my home. There is power in our words. All praise and glory belongs to You, Lord.

I would like to thank my wonderful mother, Dorrett Cambridge, for raising me and always wanting the best for me. Mom, I know you have questioned whether you were a good mother. Well, I want to publicly honor you. You are an awesome mother. Regardless of what's happened in the past, it will never negate or change my love for you.

To my two big brothers, Steven and Donald, you are very dear to my heart. Although we don't talk as often as we'd like, I appreciate the fact we never end a conversation or leave each other's presence without saying, "I love you." This is a priceless habit and I never want it to end.

I would like to thank Uncle Gerald and Aunt Jennifer Grant. You both have always been there for me, and I want you to know how much I appreciate your stabilizing force in my life. From graduations, awards ceremonies, and sitting next to me in the hospital room when I experienced a Lupus flare. Thank you, most of all, for always being the voice of reason in my life. I greatly appreciate you.

I would also like to thank my two spiritual mothers: Pearlie Berryhill and Mary Russell.

Sister Pearlie, since I was 14, you have been a great example of a Godly woman in my life. Words cannot express the gratitude I have toward you. You picked me up faithfully for church every Sunday. I can't help but giggle when I think about one Sunday you arrived at my house. I came outside in shorts and you insisted I go back in the house and change. We have had many priceless moments I will never forget. I will always be grateful for your influence in my life. Thank you for accepting me and making me part of the Steadman-Berryhill family.

Mary Russell, I adopted myself into your family and you accepted me as your daughter. From the first day we met at nail shop, I knew you were a godly woman. We further talked and realized that we attended the same church. We have been connected at the hip since then. We formed a bond that is unbreakable. I know God has something great in store for you!

Lakeisha Dixon, the baby has been born, girl! Thank you for being such a great friend throughout the years. We have had each other's back since middle school and I will always be grateful for every time you prayed, cried, laughed, and rescued me (wink).

Jolonda Rudolph, thanks for all your support and prayers. We were not childhood friends, but it definitely feels as if we were. I appreciate you for all the encouraging words and prayers. You are my forever friend.

Hasina, thanks for being a good friend through the years. You have been there for me at my lowest physical state, and I so appreciate you!

Pastor Cecil and Lady Benza Lamb, the Word you give is always dynamic! I give God praise for placing me under seasoned saints and giving me such a great spiritual foundation.

Bishop James and Jacqueline Wright, Truth Worship Center is like my second church home. This ministry has inspired and motivated me in more ways than I can express. May God continue to bless your ministry abundantly!

Pastor Deadra and Steven Rolle, thank you for raising up righteous seed for the kingdom of God. I will never forget when I began attending Spirit of Christ Youth Ministry. I was only fourteen. Your teaching and example have been a solid foundation on which I've built my life. You guys always kept it real and genuinely wanted every one of us to succeed in life. Thank you for grounding me in biblical principles and developing me to be an effective leader.

Special thanks to Bishop Sheena Gooden and Rehoboth International Faith Center for all the prayers and support. I truly love you guys.

Bishop Joe Green and Pastor Shamique Green, I have

learned so many valuable things from your teachings and know we have been divinely connected. May God continue to richly bless you.

Special thanks to Terrance Frazier. I thank God for bringing us together. I know He has great things in store for us.

Last, but not least, I want to give a special thanks to the Spirit of Christ Center and Ministries Intercessory Prayer Team. Prayer is my rock and this book would not have been possible without every one of you.

ᚙ Foreword ᚙ

7 am truly honored to be writing this foreword endorsing Susan Cambridge and her book, *The Process*. As an ordained minister, author, and certified life coach, God has given me spiritual discernment. I recognize when there is power and anointing in a place, person, or thing. In order for you to have a testimony in an area, you must have gone through the fire and still have the scars to prove it. Minister Susan Cambridge lacks no power in the freedom of deliverance. She openly shares her life experiences to move God's people out of bondage and into a place of breakthrough in their mind, body, soul, and spirit. Susan is not only qualified to write a book on deliverance, healing, and restoration, but she has also been divinely appointed, approved, and anointed by God to be a trailblazer for others, lighting the path for the next generation to follow.

Many would have been ashamed to tackle this sensitive message, but when someone knows they have been called by God to impact and transform the nations, they obey. These special souls step out of the natural and into the supernatural. They become a modern day Moses.

Susan asked God, "Who shall I say sent me?"

God replied, "I AM THAT I AM."

Just as God has used and sent Susan, He can use and send you. However, you must to be willing to go through the process of liberation. You must open your mouth and declare you are whole and begin to see yourself into a submitted position with Christ.

In this groundbreaking book, Susan walks out "the process" for individuals to operate in complete and total deliverance. There's no microwave turnaround time in this book, but this is an instruction manual designed for earnest souls to experience a net-breaking process that will revolutionize lives in the area of deliverance, healing, and restoration.

Susan Cambridge has an extraordinary gift to teach, train, mentor, and empower the body of Christ on this subject through revelation, knowledge, wisdom, and her personal experiences. Be prepared to read each chapter again and again as God begins to break up the ground in your heart and lay the foundation He has for your life. Get ready to walk away replenished, refreshed, and reconnected, but this time through awareness, understanding, insight, and revelation.

Join my friend Susan Cambridge on a journey you will never forget. It's your season! It's your time! It's your turn!

> Break up your unplowed ground; for it is time to seek the LORD, until he comes and showers his righteousness on you. (Hosea 10:12 NIV)

— Lakeisha Dixon, CLC, CRC
www.lakeishadixon.com

❧ Vocabulary ❧

Process:

> a natural phenomenon marking gradual changes that lead toward a particular result.

Heal:

> to make sound or whole.

Deliverance:

> the act of freeing someone or something.

Restoration:

> a bringing back to a former position or condition.

⮡ Introduction ⮢

Entry from my 2005 Journal

Angry, frustrated, hopeless and worthless. Yes, I said it. These are words that described me at this point in my life. If you were in my shoes you would feel the same way. The neglect, rejection, and the abuse that I experienced would cause anyone to give up, but I'm still here. The only problem is that I'm wounded and in desperate need of healing. You grow up not knowing who to trust, not even your church brothers and sisters, best friend or family members. Believe it or not these individuals bring most of the disappointments. But let me not forget the number one person that I should be able to trust to make good decisions concerning my life, but I don't. The person who continued to hurt me after knowing about what I've been through. Wow, even to this day she has not recognized that I'm crying out for help to be healed of the diseases of my soul. She continues to go on and complete her daily routines as if I don't even exist. She participates in all of the church functions and reads just about every Christian book that comes out, but she continues to hurt and neglect me. Why doesn't she talk to me? Why doesn't she pay attention to my needs like she takes care of the needs of others? Does she really think God is pleased with her? Must be because she feels anointed from time to time. What a hypocrite! At times, I attempt to let her know that I still exist and that she is neglecting me. The funny thing is that I enjoy getting in trouble because it's during that time when I feel that we are the most connected. She tends to my needs. I like that so much, but her inconsistency is so dangerous, dangerous to the point I can't trust her. Her actions have proven that she doesn't trust God and to me she is a dangerous person. Now look I'm not saying I'm spiritually politically correct but in my "book of rules" she's dangerous. Just thinking about it makes me want to scream "Suuuusssaannnn, can't you see what you are doing to me". "Can't you see that it doesn't get better if you don't allow God to heal, restore and deliver you out of bondage? It's time for the stumbling blocks to be permanently removed. You can't continue the way you are going. It's only an illusion. I'm tired of pretending. I'm tired of going through the motions in church. I'm tired of having church as usual. I need to be free, Susan. Please hear me clearly. You are not delivered.

Every time I read this entry from my journal, I get goose bumps. I penned this during my beginning process of deliverance, healing, and restoration. My life was an emotional upheaval and I was in desperate need of professional help. As a clinician, I understood the importance of emotional stability and sense of well-being, so I decided to make an appointment with a counselor. I will share more details of this experience in later chapters, but first I want to tell you how this entry came about.

Therapy

What is she going to think of me? My heart pounded in my chest. *Is she going to judge me and spread my personal business around town?* A tsunami of fears swept over me as I punched my counselor's phone number into my phone. *Maybe I should just hang up. I can't do this. I'm too embarrassed.* Negative thoughts raced through my mind as I pressed the phone to my ear. *How it is possible I need therapy? People should be coming to me!*

A gentle voice interrupted my troubled thoughts. "Good morning, this is Minister Parker. How may I help you?"

I choked over the lump lodged in my throat. I struggled to speak. "This is Susan Cambridge and I . . . I . . . I . . ."

"It's all right, Susan." The woman's soft voice on the other end of the phone reassured me. "Can you tell me how you are feeling right now?"

I did my best to stifle a sob escaping my trembling lips. "I don't know whether I'm coming or going."

My life was in shambles and I didn't know how to put it back together. I was faithful to the Lord's house, heavily involved in ministry, and attended every Christian conference I could, hoping to discover a way to be set free, but my soul remained shackled in chains. Something was missing. I thought I would make a little progress, but then I fell back into sin's pit of despair. I was drowning in a sea of hopelessness because of slipping back into a life of disobedience, rebellion, and fornication. An intense battle raged in my mind. I knew the enemy was after me, and if God didn't shatter these sinful strongholds in my life, the enemy would sift me as wheat.

"Simon, Simon, Satan has asked to sift all of you as wheat." (Luke 22:31 NIV)

Now, you may be asking, "Why didn't you stand on God's Word, fasting and believing for a mighty deliverance?"

I did all that. I repented and confessed my deliverance. The Holy Spirit freed me each time, but there was one dilemma. I lacked teaching on how to keep my spiritual house clean. I kept opening the door to unclean guests.

I was relieved when Minister Parker scheduled an appointment for me that same week. Something was different this time. I knew the process had begun.

Blast from the Past

The therapist listened patiently as I shared a portion of my life's story. In soothing tones she said, "Susan, you have an inability to connect with things in your past."

This was a challenge for me therapeutically. I shared specific details with incongruent affect and mood. For example, I appeared happy when specific events warranted me to be upset or sad. Therapeutically, this would be considered inappropriate or incongruent affect as it relates to the current mood. My therapist explained to me I was disconnected from my feelings and had a type of unhealthy detachment. There were certain areas in my life where I was completely numb. Although I claimed on many occasions these things didn't bother me, my therapist wasn't convinced. As a result, I became defensive and challenged her clinical assessment, but deep down in my heart I knew she was right and believed God had put her in my life for a reason.

"Susan, if you want to be healed from your painful past, you must be honest with yourself and release the fear associated with reconnecting with your feelings." My therapist explained more about the importance of reconnecting with my feelings and allowing God to heal my inner child. She encouraged me to pray and ask God to help me locate those areas where I needed healing and connect with the part of myself I was ashamed of. I prayed and prayed because I desperately longed to be healed and restored. I knew if I didn't get help, I would continue traveling down a destructive path that would lead to disastrous consequences.

Homework

One of my homework assignments was to keep a daily journal, jotting down my thoughts for each day. In the beginning this was very difficult for me. My journal entries were shallow. I couldn't jot down my feelings until God finally gave me a breakthrough.

One night I tossed and turned. Finally in desperation I cried out to the Lord, "What are you trying to tell me?"

I plopped down on a chair at the dining room table, opened my journal, and began to write. When I completed my journal entry, I was crying uncontrollably. I picked up my telephone and called my therapist, not realizing it was two o'clock in the morning.

In a groggy voice, my therapist responded, "Susan, now you have connected to your feelings."

The entry you read at the beginning of the Introduction was what I wrote in my journal that night. From that moment forward, my healing process began, and I was on my way to freedom.

Written for You

This book is written specifically for people are who are tired of dealing with the demons from their past and long for complete freedom and wholeness. If that's you, I promise you will not be disappointed. This book was birthed out of intense prayer and pain. The emotional pain I experienced led me to seek God on a greater level. It was important to me to find out what was causing such anguish and bitterness in my heart. This journey was emotional and difficult, but I knew if I pressed into that secret place in God, I would find what I was looking for.

By no means am I saying this book is the complete blueprint on deliverance and restoration. I am only sharing how God led me. However, I can reassure you this book will help you understand God's plan and purposes for your life are good and not of evil. They are to give you a future and a hope. This future doesn't consist of depression, rejection, or lack, but happiness and freedom. I believe my personal story will encourage and motivate you to seek God on a higher level, leading you on a path of healing, deliverance, and restoration. He is the healer of the brokenhearted. I pray my transparency will encourage you. If God granted me an inner miracle, He will grant you one, too.

> Then Peter began to speak: "I now realize how true it is that God does not show favoritism." (Acts 10:34 NIV)

Keep a Journal Handy

When I went through my deliverance process, I kept a journal to capture my daily thoughts and complete assignments from my therapist. As you read this book, keep a notebook or journal handy because I'm going to ask you to identify specific things and write them down. Since I kept my journal with me at all times, I preferred to have a notebook with loose leaf paper inside. I didn't use a typical journal because people are nosey and sometimes the word *journal* causes them to get sticky fingers. Your thoughts are personal and should be for your eyes only unless you are spiritually led to share with others. Maintain your confidentiality as much as you can. It is not wise for your personal information to get out without your consent.

If you are still reading at this point, this book is a divine appointment with the Holy Ghost. I'm not going to tell you this journey will be easy because it wasn't for me and at times it is still challenging to maintain my deliverance, but I can tell you when this process is complete, you will have experienced the Refiner's fire. A spirit of heaviness will lift, causing your spirit man to be rejuvenated, recharged, and restored. Don't even allow the enemy to make you think you lost time and ground because you will be catapulted into a place in God that has been waiting for you!

Prayer

Dear most precious and heavenly Father, I humbly come to you and thank You for this opportunity to embark on this journey to the newfound freedom awaiting me at the end of this process. I don't know how long it may take. I don't know what to expect, but I do know the plans You have for me are good and not evil, plans to give me a future and a hope. I know beyond a shadow of a doubt this hope entails freedom. This is a freedom only You can give. This freedom is not conditional. This freedom will not keep me in bondage to my past. This freedom speaks life and not death. This freedom brings me everlasting peace. Father, keep me focused on You throughout this journey and remove every distraction that would hinder me for this is truly my season of healing, restoration, and deliverance. You love me and have not forgotten about me. I can trust Your heart because Your heart beats for me. I commit to this process and rest in Your Word. Amen.

⪧ Chapter 1 ⪦

MY STRUGGLE WITH DELIVERANCE

How did I get to this place? These words echoed through my mind as I drove to work. I wished I could have stayed home in bed, pulled the covers over my head, and cried, but I couldn't. I had to work. Hiding in my home wasn't an option.

I was drowning in confusion and defeat. Isolation made sense to me. I pulled away from everyone and created a makeshift prison in my mind. Satan didn't have to hold me hostage because I became an expert at tying chains around myself.

Negative thoughts swirled in my head. *You'll never get it right. You're a failure and not worthy to be a leader in your church, especially the singles' ministry.*

I agreed with every negative thought and feeling. My contrary reasoning superseded the Word of God, bringing more darkness to my soul. I had no "lens" of faith. Scales formed on my eyes. I couldn't see clearly. It wasn't that I didn't know the Word. I had been under great Bible teaching. Pastor Cecil Lamb from the Spirit of Christ Center and Ministries in North Miami Beach, Florida, had poured a solid, biblical foundation into my soul, but something was keeping me from walking in victory.

I was recognized as an up-and-coming leader. I worked diligently in ministry, but I soon discovered "busyness" was the problem. I was so involved in the work of the Lord I neglected my physical, mental, and spiritual needs.

Lupus

I was only 13 when I was diagnosed with Lupus. Battling the disease for more than twenty years, I had experienced several major complications: pneumonia, blood clots, kidney infections, lupus flares, gallbladder, and heart surgery. Hospitalizations were lengthy and frequent.

Some days the pain was excruciating and I wanted to die. I questioned why God allowed me to go through this sickness and pain at such a young age. My heart was heavy during this difficult time. I was dealing not only with the disease but also with severe depression. The physical trial was bad enough, but then the emotional trauma made everything worse. A side effect of my medications was depression, but I knew the fog covering my mind was coming from a deeper place within.

Digging Deeper

My therapist delved deeper to help me uncover the cause for my depression. The weekly sessions became more intense. She asked me to complete several activities and discussed my relationship with my father. Initially, I shared how I was a daddy's girl and looked forward to spending quality time with him when I was a little girl. My favorite childhood memories were when he picked me up every other weekend. We went fishing and shopped for books at the Swap Shop Outdoor Flea Markets.

My therapist leaned in closer and asked, "Do you speak with your father now?"

Scalding tears stung my eyes. I shook my head and gasped, "No!"

Daddy's Girl

September 23, 1996, was the day my relationship with my father changed forever. I was anxiously waiting by the phone for my father to call and wish me a happy birthday, but the call never came. I didn't speak to him for several weeks. One day I found the courage to call and ask him why he didn't call me for my birthday.

He replied, "I forgot."

My heart sunk and I didn't know what to say. I was devastated, but I dismissed it and put the incident in the back of my mind.

The following year I graduated from high school. I was so eager to see my dad at the graduation ceremony, but he never showed up. I couldn't understand it. My father never missed a birthday, Christmas, or any other significant event in my life. Rejection set in. I loved my father and believed he loved me, but I was severely wounded.

I tried to explain my feelings to my therapist. "Since those two incidents, our relationship has changed significantly."

"I can understand your feelings." My therapist jotted down a few notes and then looked up at me. "Did you have any contact after he failed to show up at your graduation?"

My head bobbed. "Yes, we did speak infrequently on the phone, but it was because he wanted me to call his mistress to tell her something."

"Did you say 'mistress?'"

"Yes, my father left my mother for another woman. Then he married my stepmother and began dating another woman simultaneously." I had no problem vocalizing my past hurts. "At that time, it really didn't bother me because I had his attention, but when he started neglecting me, I became very jealous."

After my counselor listened intently, she said, "Susan, I want you to share with me some of the other disappointments you have experienced with your father."

I didn't have to think very long before more painful memories waltzed through my head. I wondered what good all my venting was doing. I soon found out.

☙ Chapter 2 ☙

BLAST FROM THE PAST

I shared with my therapist one incident I remembered vividly. One Fourth of July I asked my father to buy me some fireworks, but he refused. Later on that same day he picked me up and took me to his girlfriend's house to light fireworks with her children. I was so hurt and was convinced he loved and cared more for her kids than me.

Satan was using rejection, hurt, and neglect to shape my young soul. He was determined to destroy my life and orchestrated his evil plan by sowing seeds of hurt and low self-esteem in my heart. All the bad "seed" from my father's disregard grew into a deep insecurity. I looked for love in all the wrong places. I hungered for male attention, and it didn't matter what it cost me.

Emotional Tug-of-War

As Minister Parker probed deeper about my father's relationships, I felt myself emotionally detaching and shutting down. I became completely silent and was too embarrassed to share any more of my painful past. An emotional tug-of-war ensued. I knew I had to share memories I hoped I'd forget. It was vital to my healing. If I didn't deal with all the baggage I was carrying, it would deal with me. (I had enough luggage to go around the world—twice!) For the first time in my life, my desire to be well was greater than my pain. I was determined to be delivered and healed. The time had come for me to start unpacking.

Moral Compass

The Bible is our moral compass. It is filled with truths that can set us free. I was pleasantly surprised when I read about another servant of the Lord hiding among some baggage.

So they asked the LORD, "Where is he?"

And the LORD replied, "He is hiding among the baggage." (1 Samuel 10:22 NLT)

Shortly after Saul had been anointed by the prophet Samuel to be king, the people couldn't find him anywhere. They asked the Lord to show them where he was, and the Lord revealed to them that he was hiding among the baggage.

I sure could relate to Saul. Emotional baggage is very cumbersome and hinders us from being what the Lord wants us to be. After limping through several therapy sessions, I knew God was asking me to stop hiding among the baggage of my past. There was only one place for the bags of my past—the foot of the cross. Jesus was there with His arms wide open, ready, and willing to help me unpack.

Unpacking Begins

As the unpacking began, I realized my decisions and actions were a direct result of the abandonment and rejection I had experienced. I understood why the Bible stresses the importance of parents being responsible for the upbringing of their children, but there also comes a point when children grow up and must take responsibility for their actions. They can't continue to live year by year making excuses for bad behavior.

I knew the Lord was shining His light in the nooks and crevices of my soul. There was no more room for excuses because my destructive behaviors were not affecting just me—they were affecting other people. I hadn't dealt with these issues and they were bleeding into other areas of my life. It was time to stop the hemorrhaging. I believed if just one sliver of Calvary's cross was inserted in my bleeding heart, it would beat again.

May We Talk?

Writing this chapter has been a struggle. I don't enjoy revisiting the dark moments in my life. Any level of transparency makes us vulnerable, but I have been set free by the blood of Jesus from all the powers of darkness. I write this book with confidence that every reader will be encouraged and know they are not alone. One of the enemy's tactics is to make us feel as though we are all alone, but remember he is the father of lies and a defeated foe. I'm living proof God can set us free. Has this process been easy? No, but I thank God daily for my process of healing, deliverance, and restoration.

Blame Game

Because of the abandonment and rejection I felt from my father, I built up a level of resentment and bitterness toward my mother. In my mind, she was responsible for my father leaving. I found myself thinking, *If only she had acted properly, he would have never left us.* As I grew older, I understood there was more to the story than I was privy to at that time, but I subconsciously blamed her.

Therapy helped me recognize I was harboring negative feelings in my heart against certain individuals. Some of these things I will not disclose for confidentiality purposes, but I will share I held my mother accountable for things she was not responsible for. When my relationship with my father began deteriorating, I expected her to fill that void. I longed for intimate mother-daughter talks and wanted to snuggle with her while we watched television. I wanted to be nurtured. Please don't get me wrong, by no means am I saying or implicating my mother was an unfit parent. In reality, my mother was wonderful! She did the best she could, but I had to learn everybody's love language is different. My mother showed her love for me by being a provider, protector, and supporter. Is our relationship perfect? Absolutely not. But we love each other and are dedicated to pursuing a healthy relationship.

If you need help, I encourage you to find someone to help you unpack. As you become healthy, you will pursue healthy relationships with those you love. Start unpacking today.

᚛ Chapter 3 ᚜

THE ACCUSER OF THE BRETHREN

*T*hen I heard a loud voice shouting across the heavens,

> "It has come at last—salvation and power and the Kingdom of our God, and the authority of his Christ. For the accuser of our brothers and sisters has been thrown down to earth—the one who accuses them before our God day and night. (Revelation 12:10 NIV)

My therapist and I continued to meet twice a week. The first couple of months I dreaded the sessions. Satan tormented me with suffocating guilt, constantly reminding me about past mistakes and people I had wounded. I was the enemy's

"Amen Corner." I agreed with every condemning thought he whispered in my ear. I felt as if I was carrying heavy weights on my back. Oppressed and defeated, a spirit of depression affected every part of my life, especially my relationships.

Toxic Relationships

I was inept at keeping healthy relationships. Everyone labeled me as being "needy." I required a lot of attention, and when I didn't get it, I would get extremely upset and send everyone on guilt trips. In my twisted thinking, I felt individuals were rejecting me. I was so insecure I needed constant reassurance and reminders I was loved and on good terms with those I cared about. The more depressed I became, the more toxic my relationships were.

At times, people took advantage of my vulnerability. They used and abused me verbally and physically. Keep in my mind, during this difficult period in my life, I was an active member of my church and loved the Lord, but there were holes in my soul. I was searching for love in all the wrong places. I looked to people to fill the holes, but only Jesus could satisfy my soul. During these "wilderness" years, I finally came to the place where I wanted to be set free more than anything else in the world.

Coming to a Head

As I cried out to the Lord for deliverance, He allowed two major incidents to take place, revealing to me I had some major issues that had to be dealt with. The scales were beginning to fall off my eyes.

I began dating a Marine when I was twenty-five. He was very nice and respectful, and I enjoyed his company. He was originally from Miami but was stationed at Camp Lejeune in Jacksonville, North Carolina. On the initial visit, my two best friends accompanied me and we had a great time. I dreamed of becoming his wife, completely ignoring the fact he was already married. In my mind, I justified dating him because he and his wife were separated. I don't recall him ever mentioning they were planning on getting a divorce. Nevertheless, we talked daily for a few months, and then the calls became less frequent. Insecurity set in and I thought somebody else was in the picture. Things seemed different between us and I wanted the truth. He reassured me it was all in my head and he wanted to be with only me. He mailed me a money order and told me to book a ticket and fly back to North Carolina.

My best friend, Lakeisha, called me the night before I was scheduled to leave. "Susan, I am not comfortable with you taking this trip by yourself."

My will was set. Since she didn't give a concrete reason why I shouldn't go, I dismissed her concerns and took the trip, determined not to regret it.

My boyfriend picked me up from the airport. The two-hour drive from Raleigh to Jacksonville was awkward and distant. Uneasiness settled in and I felt something wasn't right. The next morning when he went to work and I was left alone at his house, I rummaged through his stuff. My actions were typical behavior of an insecure individual.

What I found was unbelievable! The love letters from other women were just beginning of our problems. I discovered cocaine, marijuana, scales, and other drug paraphernalia. I was petrified.

My mind was buzzing. *I've got to call Lakeisha! I am going to get arrested and thrown in jail.*

Lakeisha was just as stunned as I was. "Susan, you must get back home immediately!"

Excuses formed in my head. *You can't leave yet. Your flight doesn't leave for two days.* I think I had been reading too many urban Black books because stranger thoughts swarmed in my head. *Maybe he can take me shopping since he has drug money.*

When he returned home, I confronted him about the letters. Ironically, I didn't sense an urgency to mention the drugs first. He sat me down and informed me he didn't think our relationship was working. "Susan, I want to be just friends."

I was livid. "What do you mean you want to be just friends? Did you fly me to another state to inform me you no longer want to be with me?"

He nodded his head and stared at me blankly.

I bolted to the kitchen, picked up a knife, and chased him around the house. He raced outside and I ran behind him, wearing only a shirt and panties and screaming like a lunatic. A few minutes later, I fell to the ground, howling. He came, picked me up, and led me back into the house. Then he gave me some marijuana to smoke to calm my nerves.

I think you can see my point. My emotional instability led me to make irrational decisions that could have landed me in jail because military laws are even stricter than civilian laws.

Praise Break

Even writing about it sends shivers up and down my

spine. I see how God had His hand on me. I need to take a moment and thank Him for His grace and mercy. Hallelujah! Father God, You are awesome. Your hands were upon me even in the midst of sin. You are worthy of praise and honor. Where would I be if You weren't on my side? I'm so every grateful and make a vow to praise and worship You until my last breath.

What if the LORD had not been on our side? (Psalm 124:1 NLT)

When I returned home, my mother greeted me at the airport. She held me as I cried in her arms. I have always appreciated how my mother loves me unconditionally. She allowed me to talk about what happened when I was ready, and I was very grateful.

After the Marine and I broke up, I fell into a deeper depression and even struggled with suicidal thoughts. The pressures of life weighed me down, and I felt I had no strength to recover.

Purpose

My purpose for sharing my personal struggles with you is to assure you that you are not alone. Countless individuals are struggling with sensitive issues and feel as if no one understands or even cares. Some of these issues have stigmas associated with them and cause embarrassment and shame. This keeps people from seeking spiritual counsel and getting the help they need. I am so thankful I was introduced to Jesus. You may already know Him, but allow me to brag on His goodness. He sticks closer than a brother. He keeps my secrets confidential and collects my tears in a jar. He comforts me in the midnight hour and accepts me for who I am. He gives me divine wisdom and leads me into all truth. One of the greatest things I love about Jesus is that He is triune. He consists of three persons: the Father, Son, and Holy Ghost. Once I accepted Jesus in my heart as Lord and personal Savior, it reunited me with my Father and the Holy Ghost.

In addition to being reunited with my heavenly Father, my relationship with Him granted me full access to use His authority on earth as it is in heaven. This authority equipped me with one of the greatest weapons against the enemy—the blood of Jesus. When I finally realized the sanctity of my lineage, I became unstoppable and broke the stronghold of depression that had plagued me for years. Through prayer, worship, and spiritual guidance, I became stronger and walked in the confidence of knowing everything would work together for good to those who love the Lord and are called accordingly to His purpose. This process was a journey toward healing, restoration, and deliverance. It didn't happen overnight, but I found my Father to be faithful and He did heal, restore, and deliver me.

Your struggle may not be with depression or rejection. Perhaps you struggle with gambling, pornography, perversion, or pride. Regardless of what your issues are, God loves you and desires for you to be free. The God who works behind the scenes, sees behind your heart. Your season has come. You have not been forgotten. The fact you are reading my book proves to me God has His hand on you. He wants to set you free and break every chain binding you. Open your heart and allow God to take you through your own personal journey. You will not be disappointed with the results.

So if the Son sets you free, you are truly free. (John 8:36 NLT)

⁐ Chapter 4 ⁐

REDEFINING MOMENT

May 15, 2010, was a redefining moment in my life. I attended the Women with a Vision 2010 Conference at the Spirit of Christ Church. It was a phenomenal. The speakers were dynamic and the Word was timely. God knew what I needed to hear.

A few weeks later I was asked to give my testimony at our annual luncheon. Initially, I was hesitant and wished they would invite someone else to share, but the Holy Spirit dealt with me about being authentic. "Susan, I want you to share some of your past hurts."

I dismissed what the Lord was asking me to do and started negotiating testimonies. "Father, I have plenty to share about healing and financial provision. Let me tell them about the doors of job opportunities You have opened for me, but please don't ask me to share deep personal issues and the things I want to keep secret."

I had no peace about sharing my "safe" testimonies. The Holy Spirit continued speaking to me. "Susan, prosperity in the soul is just as important as prospering financially and physically! I will use your story to bring health to souls of hurting women, and while you share, I will bring health to your soul too."

I was petrified! My heart thumped loudly in my chest. "But Lord, what will everyone think about me after I share all I have done and been through?" Embarrassment and shame swept over me. I immediately rebuked the spirit of fear and rejection.

"Susan, haven't I forgiven and delivered you?" His words soothed my troubled soul.

"Yes, Lord."

"There are others who need to hear what I've done for you so they can be set free too. It's time for people to know what I have done for you."

A parade of memories marched through my head. The sweetness of His presence lingered and the Holy Spirit reminded me of past victories He had given me. For years I had asked the Lord to change me and help me grow in my faith. I had prayed a long time for prosperity in my soul. During those difficult days, I attempted to find peace and joy in all the wrong places. My unstable emotions reigned, and I made many poor choices.

The Soul

The soul's components consist of our mind, will,

emotions, and intellect. We have to keep all four of these under subjection to our spirit. The Bible tells us how to do this.

> And do not be conformed to this world, but be ye transformed by the renewing of your mind, that you may prove what is that good and acceptable and perfect will of God. (Romans 12:2 KJV)

To renew our minds, we must take time to cultivate an intimate relationship with Jesus. It's imperative we remain in His Word and practice His presence. Communing with Him will renew our minds. When our thinking and belief systems line up with the Bible, we will be changed and exemplify Christ. The fruit of the Spirit will be evident in our lives.

Spiritual Warfare

Satan will do everything in his power to keep you from studying the Word of God and being in the Lord's presence. He knows the more we renew our minds, the more victories we will experience and the more our quality of life will improve. The presence of the Lord renders the enemy powerless. Seeking God's highest will should be our top priority because when we do, blessings follow.

> Seek ye first the kingdom of God and all His righteousness and all things shall be added unto you. (Matthew 6:33 KJV)

This scripture gives us great insight. When we seek first the kingdom of God and do things His way, He promises to supply all of our needs. And read this wonderful promise.

Delight thyself also in the LORD: and he shall give thee the desires of thine heart.to give all the desires of our heart. (Psalm 37:4 KJV)

You may be asking, "What if my desires do not add up to the Word of God?"

Remember the scripture in Romans I mentioned earlier? Paul encouraged the people to renew their minds so they could prove what the good, acceptable, and perfect will of the Lord was. When we renew our minds, God purges out irrational thinking and replaces it with the wisdom and knowledge of God.

When we seek God first and implement biblical principles in our lives, our minds will begin the process of being freed from irrational thinking. Our new thoughts will be full of the desires God wants for our lives. The negativity and unbelief will be replaced by a vibrant faith. He longs for His children to be full of the joy of the Lord.

True Prosperity

As I practiced what I was learning, my faith grew. No longer was I unstable and making poor choices, but I was growing in the ways of the Lord. My soul was prospering and God was making me into a vessel of honor for His kingdom.

Beloved, I pray that you may prosper in all things and be in health, just as your soul prospers. (3 John 1:2)

God loves to see us grow in our faith. He is pleased when our souls prosper. He wants our emotions to be healthy. Dysfunctional lives do not bring glory to Him. We shouldn't be unstable—our lives should be built upon the Solid Rock.

Our heavenly Father has provided the Prince of Peace for our lives. He has given us a peace that surpasses all understanding that will guard our hearts and minds through Christ Jesus.

Ready or Not

The Lord was so faithful to walk with me through all my doubts and questions. Once I had those settled, I was willing to remove my mask and share from my heart.

~ Chapter 5 ~

REMOVING THE MASK

*T*he moment had arrived. It was time to share my testimony publically. My heart raced and the palms of my hands were sweaty. When the speaker announced my name, I stood to my feet and trudged toward the podium. It felt like the longest walk of my life. After I arrived at the microphone, I whispered a prayer, took a big deep breath, and shared from my heart. I tried not to look into the eyes of those listening but couldn't avoid noticing some of their reactions. A few people sat mesmerized, soaking in every word. Others looked surprised, and a few even laughed. When I finished sharing, I walked numbly back to sit by my sister. For a few seconds I was so overcome with deep feelings of vulnerability I didn't notice the thunderous applause. My emotions were all over the map. I felt as if every issue I had struggled with were posted with neon signs all over my clothes. I turned from all the powerful negative emotions and thanked God for giving me the courage to share my own personal journey with Jesus. After the luncheon several people went out of their way to find me. They thanked me for sharing my story because they could relate to my struggles.

Masquerade

Have you ever worn a mask? If so, you may have concluded disguises can be fun, especially at a masquerade ball. Everyone is all dressed up wearing their nice masks and trying to figure out who's who. It's fun for a little while, but at some point, you are ready to take your mask off because it's not who you really are.

Many of us wear a mask every day. We've become an expert at pretending. Many types of issues can prompt us to try to conceal our true identity. Most people are not going to walk around and introduce themselves as Joe the Gambler or Mary the Adulterer.

You may be asking, "What are some of the ways we wear masks?" Here are a few examples.

- ✓ **Financially**—People attempt financial suicide by living the life of the rich and famous when, in fact, their situation is completely opposite. They don't have anything in the bank and live from paycheck to paycheck.

- ✓ **Holy Matrimony**—Couples brag in public about having a great marriage, but in the privacy of their homes, they call each other derogatory names and sometimes even experience domestic violence.

✓ **Church Leadership**—The church is not exempt from hypocrisy. We have those who lead the praise team on Sunday morning committing fornication on Friday night.

I do not offer these insights to condemn anyone but to help us see how the enemy sets traps and then makes us sin's slave. I know these examples are true because I wore a mask most of my life until Jesus set me free. Even though I was plagued with deep personal issues and a sinful lifestyle, for some reason I didn't resign from my church leadership responsibilities. In hindsight, I realize I should have stepped down, but I didn't. I continued serving as the singles' ministry leader and youth leader at my church.

Compromise

Before I go on, I want to be sure you understand the heart of our Father. When we repent, He forgives all our wrong doing. He remembers our sins no more. As a seasoned saint used to say, "He throws our sins into the deepest sea and puts up a 'No Fishing' sign."

But the Bible has a benchmark for leaders in the body of Christ. They abide by a different standard. They are to live pure lives. The ministry is holy and sacred. The prophet Isaiah puts it this way.

Be ye clean, that bear the vessels of the LORD. (Isaiah 52:11 KJV)

When we operate in any leadership capacity in the body of Christ, whether it be a musician, Sunday school teacher, usher, deacon, parking attendant, or church custodian, our life needs to line up with God's Word. When we are living in sin, we are disrespecting the things of God. Our sins short-circuit the power of God and hinder the flow of the Spirit. I've often wondered if this could be the reason for unanswered prayers and powerless Christianity. Are too many of God's people compromising the things of God and expecting the blessings of God at the same time?

If you are a leader in your church and are not living in submission to God's Word, immediately inform your leadership that you need to take some time off and get your house in order. Disclosing the details of your situation is a personal decision. Telling those who are over you in the Lord you are having some spiritual struggles and need to take care of them should suffice.

My Experience

When I finally accepted that God had a purpose and plan for my life, I became sensitive to the things of God and keenly aware I didn't want to compromise the anointing on my life. I realized my spiritual gifts and talents were not only for me but also for the body of Christ. This light in my soul catapulted me into wisdom. I wanted my life to be biblically grounded so I would be a vessel meet for the Master's use.

> If a man therefore purge himself from these, he shall be a vessel unto honour, sanctified, and meet for the master's use, and prepared unto every good work. (2 Timothy 2:21 KJV)

Masquerade or Inaugural Ball

When we are bound by sin, it is impossible to operate at our full spiritual capacity. We have a form of godliness but deny its power. (2 Timothy 3:5)

We want the power of God operating in every area of our lives. The graveyards are full of potential, but the people are dead. We must refuse to leave this earth without fulfilling the plan and purposes of God for our lives to maximum potential. We have the authority to decree and declare whatever we want to happen on this earth and live in the fullness of God. Why settle for attending only masquerade balls when we can have our own inauguration ball?

I'm a firm believer experience is not the best teacher. We need to humble ourselves and listen to those who have experienced these things and learn from their mistakes. If you don't know anyone who has struggles similar to yours, let me introduce myself to you. My name is Susan Cambridge and I struggled with depression, rejection, and perversion. God healed, delivered, and restored me. I invite you to learn from my past mistakes.

If our issues go unresolved, we eventually self-destruct and our lives unravel. We can wear a mask for only so long, whether it is a day, month, or several years. There comes a day when the mask must come off whether we like it or not.

When the mask comes off, what will we see? Will w exemplify Christ? Even if we won't, there is no need to hʲ from our heavenly Father. Jesus died on the cross for ⱱ we could be restored to our rightful position with Hir don't have to pretend to be something or somebody wʳ

God wants us to be transparent before Him. He knows all of our shortcomings and accepts us for who we are. Everything God says in His Word is true.

> Being confident of this, that he who began a good work in you will carry it on to completion until the day of Christ Jesus. (Philippians 1:6 NIV)

The fact this book is in your hands and you are reading this chapter is a kingdom appointment. Our heavenly Father is offering hope and victory to you, but He needs your help. Won't you surrender your life to Him? You'll never be sorry. He will be the best Friend you'll ever have. Everything He has promised will come to pass. Cry out to Him and ask for help. He will hear and answer your prayer.

❧ Chapter 6 ❧

HOW DID I GET HERE AGAIN?

*A*s a dog returns to its vomit, so fools repeat their folly. (Proverbs 26:11)

I remember sometimes sitting on the side of my bed when I was tangled in my web of sin. Questions whirled through my mind. *How did I end up back in another dysfunctional relationship? Why do I continue to make the same mistakes over and over? How did I get here again?*

I asked myself these questions on several occasions. Each time I thought I had made progress, but I found myself once again disillusioned, hurt, ashamed, and humiliated. I had to be totally embarrassed before I would seek spiritual counsel.

Abstinence Doesn't Mean Deliverance

Have you ever missed the mark and wondered if you would ever recover? Or thought you were in a place so deep you didn't know how to get out or regain your strength? I had these dark nights of the soul. I would lie on my bedroom floor and cry out to the Lord, "If You will deliver me from this trap, I won't go back." As the days went by, I was confident I had overcome my sin problem, but I quickly learned abstinence doesn't mean deliverance.

Have you ever been there? You may feel you are in a dark place or experiencing a spiritual drought. When you pray, do you feel your prayers are unheard and bounce back? I want to encourage you to remain steadfast and unmovable in the Lord. It is during these times that you need to press into prayer and worship as never before.

> Therefore, my beloved brethren, be ye stedfast, unmoveable, always abounding in the work of the Lord, forasmuch as ye know that your labour is not in vain in the Lord. (1 Corinthians 15:58 KJV)

I searched my heart, trying to find out what had drawn me back to carnal living. I realized I was dual-natured. Since Adam and Eve's fall in the Garden of Eden, we have been cursed with fleshly appetites. Yet we are made in the image of God. There is a war raging inside us. Our spirit is willing, but our flesh is weak.

> Two natures like within my breast.
> One is foul and one is blessed.
> One I love and one I hate.
> The one I feed will dominate.
> (Author unknown)

The apostle Paul warned us about the spiritual warfare every Christian engages in. We must put on the whole armor of God so we can stand against the enemy's tactics.

> For we wrestle not against flesh and blood, but against principalities, against powers, against the rulers of the darkness of this world, against spiritual wickedness in high places. (Ephesians 6:12 KJV)

One of the worst things believers can do is to believe they no longer have to do whatever it takes to gain victory over the flesh. Saints, we are in a war! We must continually humble ourselves before our Father God and ask Him to purify our hearts and souls of ungodly things.

> The heart *is* deceitful above all *things*, and desperately wicked: who can know it? (Jeremiah 17:9 KJV)

Beloved, we have a heart problem. We desperately need a heart transplant and a blood transfusion. These timeless lyrics of the old hymn should resonate in our souls: "What can wash away my sin? Nothing but the blood of Jesus." His blood has never lost its power and still provides deliverance today.

When our lives have been "altered by the altar," we live careful lives. Don't misunderstand me. We shouldn't live in fear, but we should have the fear of the Lord and never want to displease Him. Our lives should bring glory and honor to the Lord. Absolute purity and absolute humility must radiate from us.

If we have been set free from some sinful desire, we must live close to Jesus because the Bible teaches the enemy will come back to see if we are delivered.

Then it goes and takes with it seven other spirits more wicked than itself, and they go in and live there. And the final condition of that person is worse than the first. That is how it will be with this wicked generation. (Matthew 12:45 NIV)

When we have been delivered from something, whether drugs and alcohol, pornography, gambling, lying, or any other sinful act, it's imperative we refrain from putting ourselves in situations that cause us to fall in that area again. For example, drug treatment programs live by the principle that you must change people, places, and things to remain sober. So we must make abrupt changes in our lives. We can't hang around our old crowd of friends anymore. We can't sit and watch our favorite television show if it feeds the carnal nature in our soul. Believer, we must starve those fleshly appetites!

Gates to the Soul

There are gates to our souls the enemy attempts to enter through. The first is the "Eye Gate." We must be careful what we watch. Television is not what it used to be. We don't see family friendly broadcasts like *The Cosby Show* or *Good Times*. Most "reality" shows promote lust, sex, and materialism. We must develop safeguards and guard our "Eye Gate."

Remember we want our lives lined up with God's Word. Does the Bible support our theory about the "Eye Gate?" I believe it does. When Satan tempted Eve, she "saw" the fruit of the tree was good for food and it was pleasing to her eyes.

When the woman saw that the fruit of the tree was good for food and pleasing to the eye, and also desirable for gaining wisdom, she took some and

HOW DID I GET HERE AGAIN?

ate it. She also gave some to her husband, who was with her, and he ate it. (Genesis 3:6 NIV)

There is also an "Ear Gate." As believers we must be careful what we listen to. We can learn a lot from Eve's fall in the Garden of Eden. She listened to the serpent.

And finally, there is the "Feel Gate." When the serpent tempted Eve, she felt if she ate of the fruit she would be like God. We cannot allow feelings to rule our lives. Emotions fluctuate, but Jesus Christ is the same yesterday, today, and forever.

Guarding our "Soul Gates" and implementing safeguards is extremely important to maintaining deliverance from sin. Safeguards are precautionary measures we take to prevent backsliding. Repentance is the gateway to freedom. The Bible teaches when we thoroughly repent, carefulness will reign in us along with a great desire to be cleared of all wrong. This is an area I pay very close attention to because of the unnecessary setbacks I experienced. If I knew then what I know now, many heartaches would have been prevented.

For behold this selfsame thing, that ye sorrowed after a godly sort, what carefulness it wrought in you, yea, *what* clearing of yourselves, yea, *what* indignation, yea, *what* fear, yea, *what* vehement desire, yea, *what* zeal, yea, *what* revenge! In all *things* ye have approved yourselves to be clear in this matter. (2 Corinthians 7:11 KJV)

Guard the gates, saints! Your eternity depends on it.

᪥ Chapter 7 ᪥

BOUNDARIES

Setting boundaries is essential if we want to make progress in our spiritual life. Creating healthy margins will protect us from sinful habits and addictions. Unhealthy boundaries cause deep emotional pain laced with shame and depression. They can even cause diseases in our bodies. Implementing no boundaries will allow anyone and everyone in your home, even unwelcome guests. We need boundaries.

We must draw a line in the sand and be careful what we watch on television. We discussed in the previous chapter how most of Hollywood is infiltrated with lust, sex, and materialism. Many people do not understand how television shows can be so influential. I think the Lord has given me a creative way to explain this.

Have you ever watched a Burger King commercial advertising a juicy whopper with cheese and find yourself craving a whopper two days later? This same principle applies to everything we watch. If we are not careful, we can develop an appetite for something not good for us. What do we do when we are hungry? The answer is simple. We eat!

I don't like watching sensual romance movies because suddenly I am tempted to engage in lustful behavior. I have made a conscious decision to separate from anything that could possibly hinder me from being in the will of God, especially while I'm in a single state. Satan tempted Jesus on the Mount with the lust of the eyes, lust of the flesh, and the pride of life. We must be very careful.

> Therefore, "Come out from them and be separate, says the Lord. Touch no unclean thing, and I will receive you." (2 Corinthians 6:17 NIV)

If you struggle with lust, be very careful about the movies you watch. If you know you have issues with rejection and low esteem, why would you watch a show call *Cheaters?* When we feed our carnal nature, it will grow. We must starve it and build up our spiritual man. Deliverance will come if we walk in obedience to God's Word. After we are washed, cleansed, and delivered, then we will have a challenge in maintaining our deliverance, but God has given us tools in our toolbox to help us.

Fasting Instead of Feasting

Fasting is one of the weapons in our spiritual arsenal overlooked by the Church. It plays a major role along the deliverance process. This discipline helps shift our attention off ourselves and focus totally on our Deliverer. Prayer and fasting go together. There is something about this dynamic duo that moves the heart of God, and all of heaven rushes to earth to answer the needs of the seeker.

> "*Is* this not the fast that I have chosen: To loose the bonds of wickedness, To undo the heavy burdens, To let the oppressed go free, And that you break every yoke? *Is it* not to share your bread with the hungry, And that you bring to your house the poor who are cast out; When you see the naked, that you cover him, And not hide yourself from your own flesh? Then your light shall break forth like the morning, Your healing shall spring forth speedily, And your righteousness shall go before you; The glory of the LORD shall be your rear guard. (Isaiah 58: 6–8)

We all have wounds in our soul that need inner healing. Have you found yourself praying for the same thing over a period of time and getting no results? Prayer and fasting are the answer. There are many opinions about fasting and how it should be done. I was helped by Jentezen Franklin's book, *Fasting*, and highly recommend it. Pastor Jentezen does an awesome job of explaining this spiritual discipline and why it is necessary for every believer.

Biblical Examples of Fasting

There are many examples in the Bible that illustrate people seeking God for answers through fasting and praying. Let's look at a few of these.

And she wrote letters in Ahab's name, sealed *them* with his seal, and sent the letters to the elders and the nobles who *were* dwelling in the city with Naboth. She wrote in the letters, saying, Proclaim a fast, and seat Naboth with high honor among the people; and seat two men, scoundrels, before him to bear witness against him, saying, "You have blasphemed God and the king." *Then* take him out, and stone him, that he may die. (1 Kings 21:3–10)

And Jehoshaphat feared, and set himself to seek the LORD, and proclaimed a fast throughout all Judah. (2 Chronicles 20:3)

Now in the church that was at Antioch there were certain prophets and teachers: Barnabas, Simeon who was called Niger, Lucius of Cyrene, Manaen who had been brought up with Herod the tetrarch, and Saul. As they ministered to the Lord and fasted, the Holy Spirit said, "Now separate to Me Barnabas and Saul for the work to which I have called them." Then, having fasted and prayed, and laid hands on them, they sent *them* away. (Acts 13:1–3)

Prayer and fasting are biblical principles in God's kingdom. These weapons of mass destruction against the enemy's workings in our lives are powerful safeguards and should be part of our walk with the Lord. When we submit our flesh in subjection to the Spirit during fasting and praying, we create a channel that gives us direct contact with God. Yes, we can speak to God at any given time and He answers. However, fasting and praying position us to always have victory. We declare that during this time, we will submit our spirit, soul, and body to the Lord for purification and guidance.

During this season of prayer, it is important to be in tuned into the voice of the Lord. The enemy will attempt to detour, distract, and confuse us about the plan and purposes God has for our lives. We must make a commitment to keep our eyes on Jesus and stay focused during this process. Let's beat on heaven's doors until we get our answers.

⁀ Chapter 8 ⁀

Past Influences

*T*he Old Testament story of Jacob is still one of the finest examples of standing in faith until the desired results come. Isaac, the father of Jacob and Esau, was quite elderly and feeble, facing his final years. The tradition of that day was for the father to pronounce a blessing over the eldest son before the father died.

> When Isaac was old and his eyes were so weak that he could no longer see, he called for Esau his older son and said to him, "My son."
>
> "Here I am," he answered.
>
> Isaac said, "I am now an old man and don't know the day of my death. Now then, get your

equipment—your quiver and bow—and go out to the open country to hunt some wild game for me. Prepare me the kind of tasty food I like and bring it to me to eat, so that I may give you my blessing before I die." (Genesis 27:1–4 NIV)

Rebekah, the mother of Jacob and Esau, overheard the conversation between Isaac and Esau. Because she favored Jacob, she went to extreme measures to be sure he received the blessing instead of Esau. Instructing Jacob to bring some young goats, she set out to make savory food for him to present to Isaac. Rebekah picked out some of Esau's garments for Jacob to wear. Since Esau was a hairy man and Jacob was not, she put the skins of the kids of the goats on his hands and on the smooth part of his neck. She schemed to dupe her husband so Jacob would resemble Esau and receive the coveted blessing.

Jacob's deceitful nature mirrored his mother's. He did as she instructed and entered his father's room dressed in smelly animal skins and presented a delicious meal to him. Let's read about it in Scripture.

So he went to his father and said, "My father."
And he said, "Here I am. Who *are* you, my son?

Jacob said to his father, "I *am* Esau your firstborn; I have done just as you told me; please arise, sit and eat of my game, that your soul may bless me." (Genesis 27:18–19)

Isaac seemed slightly suspicious because not a lot of time had passed since he gave Esau the instructions to go make him a meal. "How did you find the food so quickly, Esau?"

Slick Jacob gave God the credit by saying, "Your God was with me."

Even after Jacob blatantly lied to his father, Isaac still wasn't completely convinced. He insisted his son come closer so he could feel him to determine he was really Esau.

> Jacob went close to his father Isaac, who touched him and said, "The voice is the voice of Jacob, but the hands are the hands of Esau." He did not recognize him, for his hands were hairy like those of his brother Esau; so he proceeded to bless him. "Are you really my son Esau?" he asked.

Then he said, "My son, bring me some of your game to eat, so that I may give you my blessing."

Jacob brought it to him and he ate; and he brought some wine and he drank. Then his father Isaac said to him, "Come here, my son, and kiss me."

So he went to him and kissed him. When Isaac caught the smell of his clothes, he blessed him and said,

> "Ah, the smell of my son is like the smell of a field that the LORD has blessed. May God give you heaven's dew and earth's richness—an abundance of grain and new wine. May nations serve you and peoples bow down to you. Be lord over your brothers, and may the sons of your mother bow down to you. May those who curse you be cursed and those who bless you be blessed." (Genesis 27:22–29 NIV)

Moments after Jacob received the blessing and left his father's presence, Esau came in from his hunting, planning to present his game and savory feast to his father.

Immediately, Isaac began to tremble because he realized Jacob had deceived him.

Esau was livid. He took a long stroll down Memory Lane and had a horrific blast from the past. Previously Jacob had taken away his birthright when he came home bone tired from working in the field. He was famished and asked Jacob to feed him. Jacob agreed to do so if Esau would sell his birthright. Esau concurred and despised his birthright from that point on.

Even though Isaac had already spoken the blessing over Jacob, Esau wanted his father to pronounce a blessing over his life as well. Isaac granted his request.

> His father Isaac answered him, "Your dwelling will be away from the earth's richness, away from the dew of heaven above. You will live by the sword and you will serve your brother. But when you grow restless, you will throw his yoke from off your neck." (Genesis 27:39–40 NIV)

After all the deception, Esau hated his brother and vowed to kill him. Remember, Jacob's mother had encouraged him to deceive his father and take his brother's blessing. Although he made the final decision, it was highly encouraged by one of the most important and influential people in his life.

Life Application

Growing up in our homes, our parents had a set of principles and standards by which they governed their families. We didn't know if everything was correct, but we obeyed because we respected our parents. Some of us even carried these principles over and applied them with our own children. Parents are usually our first teachers and they don't always instill positive attributes in our lives, but I do believe many do the best they can.

I'm not sure why Rebekah would encourage her son to steal his brother's blessing, but from that point forward, he was labeled as a liar and deceiver. Many of us have had labels and hurts imposed on us, whether right, wrong, or indifferent. We had no control. Some of the events caused us to relocate and build a new life just as Jacob did.

Time passing and relocation will never fill the void in our souls. There is no substitute for peace of mind. We must come down low at our Master's feet and consecrate to him our bad childhood, poor education, past hurts, and anything else hindering us from having inner peace. No matter what we have been through, we can still have the blessing and favor of the Lord. Jacob's deception didn't stop the Lord from guiding his life and upholding the blessing. The hand of God remained on Jacob's life and gave him the opportunity to redeem himself. God is not a respecter of persons. If he did this for Jacob, He will do the same for you.

∽ Chapter 9 ∾

THE WRESTLING MATCH

*J*acob fled from Esau and was forced to start a new life in a new land. Years passed by. He married and had a family. One day Esau came to meet his younger brother. Jacob was greatly afraid and distressed. He cried out to the Lord and pled for a mighty deliverance.

> Jacob sent messengers ahead of him to his brother Esau in the land of Seir, the country of Edom. He instructed them: "This is what you are to say to my lord Esau: 'Your servant Jacob says, I have been staying with Laban and have remained there till now. I have cattle and donkeys, sheep and goats, male and female servants. Now I am sending this

message to my lord, that I may find favor in your eyes.'"

When the messengers returned to Jacob, they said, "We went to your brother Esau, and now he is coming to meet you, and four hundred men are with him."

In great fear and distress Jacob divided the people who were with him into two groups, and the flocks and herds and camels as well. He thought, "If Esau comes and attacks one group, the group that is left may escape."

Then Jacob prayed, "O God of my father Abraham, God of my father Isaac, LORD, you who said to me, 'Go back to your country and your relatives, and I will make you prosper,' I am unworthy of all the kindness and faithfulness you have shown your servant. I had only my staff when I crossed this Jordan, but now I have become two camps. Save me, I pray, from the hand of my brother Esau, for I am afraid he will come and attack me, and also the mothers with their children. But you have said, 'I will surely make you prosper and will make your descendants like the sand of the sea, which cannot be counted.'" (Genesis 32:3–13 NIV)

Jacob must have grown weary of always looking over his shoulder for his brother. Although time marched on and Jacob carved out a new life for himself and his family, fear loomed in the back of his mind. How could he possibly be at peace and walk in the prosperity of the Lord with his past behavior haunting him? Jacob knew he must settle some things with Jehovah once and for all.

One night Jacob situated his family and retreated. Immediately, a Man showed up and wrestled with him all night. When the Man realized He couldn't prevail, He touched the socket of Jacob's hip, causing it to come out of place.

> So Jacob was left alone, and a man wrestled with him till daybreak. When the man saw that he could not overpower him, he touched the socket of Jacob's hip so that his hip was wrenched as he wrestled with the man. Then the man said, "Let me go, for it is daybreak."
>
> But Jacob replied, "I will not let you go unless you bless me."
>
> The man asked him, "What is your name?"
>
> "Jacob," he answered.
>
> Then the man said, "Your name will no longer be Jacob, but Israel, because you have struggled with God and with humans and have overcome."
>
> Jacob said, "Please tell me your name."
>
> But he replied, "Why do you ask my name?" Then he blessed him there.
>
> So Jacob called the place Peniel, saying, "It is because I saw God face to face, and yet my life was spared."
>
> The sun rose above him as he passed Peniel, and he was limping because of his hip. (Genesis 32:24–31 NIV)

Midnight Cry

Pay close attention. Jacob wrestled at night. Many of you reading these words may feel you are in a dark place, unsure where you should go or where you are headed. This place makes you very uncomfortable and anxious. Confusion looms on your horizon and you desperately want God to deliver you out of your present situation. Let me be the first to express you are not alone. I have felt the same way. I functioned in a dysfunctional state, and there was no "fun" in it.

Judging from the outside, my life appeared wonderful. I graduated from college with two degrees and landed very successful jobs. Although I had challenges physically, I lived the ideal life. However, depression consumed me and thoughts of suicide plagued my mind. Looking back, I don't believe I really wanted to die, but I wanted to permanently silence the negative thoughts bombarding my mind daily. Low self-esteem, no self-worth. I felt l wasn't good enough, and suffered condemnation from my past mistakes. The father of lies was whispering untruths in my "Ear Gate" and I believed him over who the Word of God said I was in Christ. All these negative thoughts were lies from the devil and I knew that. But at that time I didn't understand how to break those strongholds and allow the Holy Spirit to renew my mind. Because of my experience, I can relate with Jacob. I'm sure he desired to make amends with his brother and live in unity, but he was caught in his own tangled web of deceit.

Unwanted Visitor

I can imagine Jacob being tired from traveling all day with his family. The minute he decided to have some alone time, some Man comes to bother him. He probably was curious and frustrated at the same time. Can you relate? At some point during the wrestling match, Jacob realized this Man had something he needed—a blessing.

The Man touched the socket of Jacob's hip, causing it to come out of place. I think it is safe to say that Jacob was fighting hurt. Have you ever been wounded so badly you could barely function and your life became difficult? I have been emotionally panged a few times with obvious injuries. Just for clarity, your emotional wounds are not always caused by someone else—you could be the perpetrator. There was one incident in particular I remember hearing the voice of the Lord: "Susan, I have given you the strength to resist the enemy."

Like many of us being caught up in the moment, I made a deliberate decision to act contrary to the Word of God. This decision had serious repercussions. I spent many nights crying. Our poor decisions can bring on mental and emotional suffering.

Despite Jacob's fatigue and injury, he clung to the Man until he received his blessing. Give God your full attention during this night season. He will give you fresh revelation and deal with matters of your heart. Not only does He want to bless you and bring you to a place of deliverance, but He is also revealing that you are stronger than you think, even at your weakest point.

We may discover that just like Jacob we have to fight even when we are hurt. I knew God had great plans for my life—and my depression wasn't part of His plan. Even in a wounded state, I pressed through the darkness until I received a total breakthrough. I want to encourage you to do the same!

Jacob continued to wrestle after he was hurt. His tenacity wouldn't allow him to give up. God is calling you to do the same. Fight and never give up. Even during crippling fatigue, there is a supernatural strength you can tap into. This will bring you through any situation in victory.

⌒ Chapter 10 ⌒

NAME CHANGE

*W*e must never forget we were created in the image and likeness of God. There is nothing weak and imperfect about our Creator. Regardless of what we have done or experienced, there is still purity within us—but we must tap into it.

When Jacob tapped into his, he experienced a redefining moment in his life. We don't know exactly what Jacob was thinking at that moment, but we do know he wanted the blessing. To be blessed means to be empowered to prosper. It's impossible to be bound and prosperous simultaneously.

Born to Climb

You have skirted this mountain long enough; turn northward. (Deuteronomy 2:3)

Aren't you tired of skirting around the same mountain? I know I am. We don't have be strapped to our past. The enemy of our soul wants to rob us of the present moment and our divine destiny. The Word of the Lord for you today is, "Saints, it's time to move forward and scale that mountain for Jesus Christ. Don't worry or fear. You were born to climb."

Our Father's Eyes

When Jacob asked the Man of God to bless him, he was saying, "Deliver me. Set me free from the past." Thus, Jacob not only got blessed, but he also received a name change.

> And He said, "Your name shall no longer be called Jacob, but Israel; for you have struggled with God and with men, and have prevailed." (Genesis 32:28)

The Man of God did the strangest thing. He asked Jacob an odd question: "What is your name?" Have you ever wondered why he asked something He already knew? The answer wasn't for the Man—it was for Jacob. He needed to recognize he identified with all the negative connotations of what his name meant—deceiver and supplanter, but God wanted him to recognize what he was through His Father's eyes. And we need to realize how God views us. He sees us through the lens of faith. He desires to make us the best version of us we could ever be.

Do you want a name change? Are you tired of people seeing you as a liar or adulterer? Do you want your past forgiven and your slate wiped clean? Cry out to God and ask Him to cleanse you from all unrighteousness. Ask Him to give you godly wisdom so you can make good choices and wise decisions.

> If we confess our sins, He is faithful and just to forgive us *our* sins and to cleanse us from all unrighteousness. (1 John 1:9)

> If any of you lacks wisdom, let him ask of God, who gives to all liberally and without reproach, and it will be given to him. (James 1:5)

God promises to forgive you for all your sins. He will impute righteousness within you. Sometimes the hardest part of scaling the mountain is forgiving ourselves, but God leads by example. If He can forgive us, we must forgive ourselves. When you enter into His presence and taste of sweet forgiveness, you will never be the same.

When Moses went up the mountain to seek the face of God concerning the Israelites, he was changed. When he returned, his face shined so bright that the people knew he had been with the Lord. It is impossible to encounter the presence of God and not be changed. We move from faith to faith and glory to glory.

> So all of us who have had that veil removed can see and reflect the glory of the Lord. And the Lord— who is the Spirit—makes us more and more like him as we are changed into his glorious image. (2 Corinthians 3:18 NLT)

Many people have to graduate from the University of Adversity before they see their need for spiritual freedom. The School of Hard Knocks is always in session. Some folks have to be pulled through a knothole to get straightened out and surrender all to Jesus.

Jesus wants to set us free and keep us from being entangled in sin's vicious web. Let's learn from others' mistakes and not have to lose our job, family, and friends to these sins that dictate our lives.

Psychiatric hospitals are filled to capacity with people who are not in their right minds. I realize some of them are predisposed to mental illness, and I sincerely pray for them. But there are others who have refused to deal with their issues, and now their issues are dealing with them. If we rebel, disregard the Word of God, and disobey His commandments, our mental health will suffer. Oh, let's allow the Holy Spirit to renew our minds. This is God's will for us.

Devour Nourishing Soul Food

Don't Leave God Alone by Hank Kunnerman changed my life. It's filled with stories of people in the Bible who refused to leave God alone. Jacob was included in this prestigious number. Their persistent cries to God changed lives and the course of history.

As believers, we need to devour nourishing soul food to keep our spirit–man strong and the flesh weak. We've already mentioned spending time in God's presence. We also have another spiritual tool—the Bible. We need to make a conscious decision to study the Word of God daily. The children of Israel needed their daily manna for sustenance and survival. We need spiritual manna for our soul's optimal health.

Years ago someone shared with me the acronym for Bible—

*B*est
*I*nstruction
*B*efore
*L*eaving
*E*arth

Everything we need to know about life is in this Book. It is our "manual" for life. King Solomon said, "There is nothing new under the sun." He is right. Lust has always been around. If we find ourselves struggling with a spirit of perversion, we should take the time to study David's life. If we are struggling with low self–esteem, we should read about Gomer and Leah. Their stories promise to inspire and offer hope. In the mirror of God's Word, we will find our reflection and the antidote for our struggles.

In a time of fatherless homes and throw away children, we can't forget to read about Ishmael, the rejected child. So many people struggle with the spirit of rejection. God's Word will minister to those with a broken heart.

There are countless examples of people in God's Word who struggled with weaknesses and persevered until they experienced a mighty deliverance. God's love is not conditional. He still loved them and His hand guided them despite their shortcomings. The one quality each one of these people had was a tender heart toward God.

To desire Him is so seek Him.
To seek Him is to find Him.
To find Him is everything.
Unknown

There is a joy unspeakable, unshakable, and unmatched by anything or anyone. This joy can only be found in Jesus. Just to know God is pleased with us and eager to reveal Himself to each one of us on a deeper level will change our minds, homes, and worlds.

When we are bound by ungodly habits, it clouds our vision and clogs our hearing and makes it difficult to walk in the confidence and boldness in the Lord. We must decide to follow Jesus implicitly and completely. He will make us more than a conqueror. We don't have to have relapses or setbacks. We are ambassador of the Lord and have full authority from heaven to be used on earth.

When the enemy starts to remind you of your past, stand your ground and remind him of his future. Identify all the victories God has given you. Name them one by one. Begin counteracting negative thoughts and feelings by verbalizing everything God has brought you from.

As I am writing this chapter, I can't help but weep before the Lord. My heart is filled with thanksgiving for how faithful and good God has been to me. He has brought you and me from a mighty long way. I can't even walk without Him holding my hand.

We must remember we were created by the Most High God and we were made in the image and likeness of God. Let's take our rightful place in His kingdom. We can begin today by worshipping God and thanking Him for choosing us to be His sons and daughters. We are the sons and daughters of God. Let's claim our inheritance. Deliverance is our inheritance. Let's walk in this freedom today!

❧ Chapter 11 ❧

Principles of the Kingdom

God can deliver us instantly from a painful past, but in most situations it takes time. He walks with us through some difficult places, but His grace is always sufficient. Obedience to God's Word is the key to victorious Christian living.

> But he said to me, "My grace is sufficient for you, for my power is made perfect in weakness." Therefore I will boast all the more gladly about my weaknesses, so that Christ's power may rest on me. (2 Corinthians 12:9 NIV)

Even after deliverance, there will be times when we find ourselves in similar situations, causing a "blast from our painful past." This place can be mental, physical, emotional, or a mix of all three. We may spiral into deep depression and experience waves of hopelessness. The enemy taunts us with condemnation and bombards our minds with negativity. He sows seeds of doubts and unbelief. He will attempt to convince us that our deliverance never happened. He hammers us about past mistakes.

We must remember Satan is the father of lies and the accuser of the brethren. He cannot tell the truth. We must believe what God's Word says about us. We are children of God. He has clothed us in His righteousness. We have been made in His image. It is true we have all sinned and fallen short, but we have repented and Jesus' blood covers our sins. We are not the people we used to be. God wants us to walk in His anointing everywhere we go.

Let's stop at this very moment and say this prayer out loud with fervency and boldness:

Father, I thank You I am a new creature in Christ Jesus. You have forgiven me of all my past sins and You remember them no more. My mind is alert. My spirit is quickened, and all distractions have been removed so I can continue this process. I thank You in advance for all the past, current, and future victories in my life. You are my Father. I'm Your very own child. Thank you. In Jesus' name, amen.

We were taught in school when gathering information, we should ask these five pertinent questions—Who? What? When? Where? Why? Who is it about? What happened? When, where, and why did it take place?

As we grow in our faith, we will be able to discern the difference between condemnation and conviction. Satan always works in a condemning way. He beats us up and makes us feel hopeless. The Holy Spirit never condemns, but convicts. Now am I not saying we should not feel bad when we make mistakes and stumble. We will feel bad. It's part of the growing process. Actually, it's a good when we have godly conviction of wrongdoing. It is a sign we have a desire to do right and walk upright before the Lord. However, if we find ourselves not having any emotional response to sin, we need to delve into God's Word and spend more time in prayer.

When we spend quality time with someone on a more intimate level, we grow fonder of this individual and want the best for him or her. We develop a genuine concern for this person. It is no different with the Lord. If we make a commitment to spend more time with Him and learn more about Him through His Word, we will gain a greater respect for His presence and desire to please Him in every way possible. Remember, this is a process.

We need to ask *who?* Who is this affecting? We know it affects God and us, but our spouse may be affected, and possibly our children or coworkers. As a visual reminder, I like to make a list of these people on a sheet of paper, and I try to keep all these assignments in a notebook. Sometimes when we think about the person or individuals our actions are hurting, we want to do better. We are inspired to say, "God, help me!" We may even ask ourselves the question, "Who hurt you?"

Oftentimes, we find ourselves inadvertently responding to things that happened to us in the past. For me, I realized my poor self-esteem and self-worth were a direct result of the rejection I received from my father. To properly deal with the hurt, I needed to thoroughly think about who was responsible for hurting me. Sometimes it wasn't just one person—it was several people. I wrote their names down. It is important that you identify the individuals who hurt you and write them down in your notebook because you will use this list when preparing for deliverance. After my father's name, I added my name on the list.

There is an important point I would like to make. We live in a society where we always want the easiest and fastest way out of our pain. I've learned we can get a cheaper gospel that teaches, "It doesn't take all that!"

The Lord has taught me that we need to do whatever it takes to bring about and maintain our deliverance. I've spent extended periods of time weeping at the altar. I've fasted and prayed for my deliverance. I've changed my circle of friends, attended counseling sessions, and never missed a church service. I knew I was in a war with my flesh and Satan. He wanted to sift me like wheat, but I knew I had an Advocate and Intercessor at the throne of God.

> "Simon, Simon, Satan has asked to sift all of you as wheat. But I have prayed for you, Simon, that your faith may not fail. And when you have turned back, strengthen your brothers." (Luke 22:31–32 NIV)

The Lord is faithful to do His part, but I believe we have a part to do too. I knew my answer and victory were to be found in the Lord's presence because His Word declares that in His presence there is fullness of joy. When I lived bound in a darkened state, I certainly did not experience any joy. I even flew to several Christian conferences around the United States just to be in the presence of God and get free, but I continued to slip back into a place of despair.

Principles of God's Kingdom

The principles of the Kingdom of God are completely opposite of the world's principles.

- If you want to be great, you must become a servant.
- The way up is down.
- The first shall be last and the last shall be first.

To get help in God's kingdom, we must come down low at the foot of the Cross. He exalts the lowly. We must empty ourselves of all pride and humble ourselves before God. The Bible is full of stories of individuals Jesus set free. One of my favorites is blind Bartimaeus.

> Then they came to Jericho. As Jesus and his disciples, together with a large crowd, were leaving the city, a blind man, Bartimaeus (which means "son of Timaeus"), was sitting by the roadside begging. When he heard that it was Jesus of Nazareth, he began to shout, "Jesus, Son of David, have mercy on me!"

Many rebuked him and told him to be quiet, but he shouted all the more, "Son of David, have mercy on me!"

Jesus stopped and said, "Call him."

So they called to the blind man, "Cheer up! On your feet! He's calling you." Throwing his cloak aside, he jumped to his feet and came to Jesus.

"What do you want me to do for you?" Jesus asked him.

The blind man said, "Rabbi, I want to see."

"Go," said Jesus, "your faith has healed you." Immediately he received his sight and followed Jesus along the road. (Mark 10:46–52 NIV)

When Bartimaeus heard it was Jesus, he cried out. Even in a blind state, a place of darkness, a state where you don't know whether you're coming or going, you will be able to recognize the voice of the Lord. He was in the right place at the right time. He couldn't see Jesus, but he knew when he was in His presence. He called out to Jesus and asked for mercy. When they warned him to be quiet, he got louder. Saints, cry out in the dark place. When the enemy bombards your mind with negative thoughts, cry out louder. When you do, just as Jesus quieted the disciples, He will quiet the demons and rescue you.

We have access to the King. Who is the King of Glory? It is the Lord strong and mighty. The Lord mighty in battle. Although we may find ourselves in a dark place, if we seek the presence of God, He will shine His light and love in that difficult place. He will ask, "What do you want me to do for you?"

☙ Chapter 12 ☙

MEPHIBOSHETH—THE POWER OF RECONCILIATION

*J*esus entered Jericho and was passing through. A man was there by the name of Zacchaeus; he was a chief tax collector and was wealthy. He wanted to see who Jesus was, but because he was short he could not see over the crowd. So he ran ahead and climbed a sycamore-fig tree to see him, since Jesus was coming that way.

When Jesus reached the spot, he looked up and said to him, "Zacchaeus, come down immediately. I must stay at your house today." So he came down at once and welcomed him gladly.

All the people saw this and began to mutter, "He has gone to be the guest of a sinner."

But Zacchaeus stood up and said to the Lord, "Look, Lord! Here and now I give half of my possessions to the poor, and if I have cheated anybody out of anything, I will pay back four times the amount."

Jesus said to him, "Today salvation has come to this house, because this man, too, is a son of Abraham. For the Son of Man came to seek and to save the lost." (Luke 19:1–10 NIV)

The story of Zacchaeus is a beautiful example of restitution. One of the first steps to deliverance, after repentance, is restitution. After we have repented of our sins and asked the Lord to forgive us, we need to right our wrongs. Clearly defining what happened and how we plan to rectify a situation is important to walking in victory.

If you took money out of your savings account without your spouse's permission and gambled it away at the casino, you need to make that right. If you purchased pornography through the internet or cable television and lied to the customer service representatives, you need to correct the offense. Maybe the reason you are continuing to lose weight is because you are purging. You must confess your secret to a godly mentor and allow him or her to speak into your life. If you neglect this important fundamental brick in your spiritual foundation, sin will continue to rule over you.

Maybe you embellish stories to manipulate people into doing what you want them to do? Humble yourself before the Lord and repent of your need to control every situation. These examples may not fit your current situation, but I am confident when you ask the Holy Spirit to reveal to you the areas of bondage in your life, He will show you. Be willing to be honest because God already knows the truth. Your defining the problem will catapult you in a position to accept that this is an issue and you need help.

Once there was a hungry soul seeking the Lord at the altar. He was so convicted by the message. As the tears of repentance flowed down his cheeks, he sobbed, "What a sinner I am! What a sinner I am!" After a few moments, the Lord showered His love upon him. He lifted his head and gave a victory shout. "Oh, what a Savior! What a Savior!"

It may be painful at first to take a good look at ourselves and the bondages in the crevices of our soul, but our loving Lord doesn't leave us there. As soon as we humble ourselves before Him, He comes running to us and shows us that His grace is always greater than our sin.

Conviction or Condemnation

We must recognize the difference between conviction and condemnation. When the Holy Spirit convicts us of our sins, we always have hope. He assures us of His forgiveness, but when the enemy of our souls comes, He condemns. We feel hopeless. We doubt God's love for us and don't feel we can be forgiven. Condemnation is never from the Lord.

> Therefore, there is now no condemnation for those who are in Christ Jesus. (Romans 8:1 NIV)

David and Jonathan

David and Jonathan had a special friendship. Jonathan was the son of King Saul and despite his father's hatred for

David, he loved him like a brother. The two friends promised whoever outlived the other would care for their families forever.

The Bible mentions the day came when Jonathan and King Saul died in a battle. The city was in an uproar. David became king and many wondered what was going to happen to them because of the changing of the guard.

> Jonathan, Saul's son had a son who was lame in his feet. He was five years old when the news about Saul and Jonathan came from Jezreel; and his nurse took him up and fled. And it happened, as she made haste to flee, that he fell and became lame in his feet. His name was Mephibosheth. (2 Samuel 4:4)

David remembered the promise he made to Jonathan. Instead of destroying the descendants of Saul and preventing them from trying to regain the throne, he actively sought to find them to show them kindness. He learned Jonathan's son Mephibosheth, was still living. David's servants found him in a city name Lodebar. This city was known for barrenness, wastelands, and desolations. Mephibosheth had lost his royal rank, prestige, and superiority. He had gone from living in the palace to the pit. No longer was he powerful, but pitiful.

David summoned Mephibosheth to come to the palace. When he entered the king's presence, he fell on his face and prostrated himself. King David said to him, "Do not fear, for I will surely show you kindness for Jonathan your father's sake, and will restore to you all the land of Saul your grandfather; and you shall eat bread at my table continually" (2 Samuel 9:7).

Mephibosheth couldn't believe what the king had said.

He replied, "What is your servant that you should look upon such a dead dog as I?" (2 Samuel 9:8).

Mephibosheth didn't understand how powerful he was because of his lineage. He compared himself to a dog. David ignored his comment and called for Saul's servant, Ziba, and said to him, "I have given to your master's son all that belonged to Saul and to all his house. You therefore, and your sons and your servants shall work the land for him, and you shall bring in the harvest, that your master's son may have food to ear. But Mephibosheth your master's son shall eat bread at my table always" (2 Samuel 9:10).

I wanted to take extra time giving you an accurate description of Mephibosheth because some of you may relate to his upbringing and living conditions. Mephibosheth was being cared for by his nurse and while fleeing from the city, she dropped him causing his crippled condition.

Webster's' dictionary defines lame as having a body part, especially a limb, so disabled as to impair freedom of movement. I can't imagine how difficult it was for Mephibosheth as a child. He probably fell many times and had no one to help him up. He wasn't living in the palace anymore so there were no maids and servants.

You may not have grown up with a physical disability like Mephibosheth, but you can relate to having an emotional disability. Someone you trusted and loved "dropped" you. They compromised your innocence or left you to be raised by the foster care system. In the midst of being raised by a foster parent, you learned one day after they dropped you off at school, they were killed in a car accident. Once again, you have been rejected. These examples may not be your exact story, but your story left you with the same thoughts and feelings as Mephibosheth. Rejection. Hopelessness. Unworthy.

I have good news! Just as King David and Jonathan promised to look after each other's families, Jesus made a promise to you.

> Then he said to them, "Thus it is written, and thus it was necessary for the Christ to suffer and to rise from the dead the third day, and that repentance and remission of sins should be preached in His name to all nations, beginning at Jerusalem. And you are witnesses of these things. Behold, I send the Promise of my father upon you; but tarry in the city of Jerusalem unto you are endued with power from on high." (Luke 24:46–49)

Jesus promised when He left the earth, He would send back the promise of the Father. He instructed his followers to tarry until they received the power from up above. Jesus understood He was sent to earth to accomplish one single purpose—to reunite us with our eternal Father. He knew we would sin. He also knew one day we would be faced with trials and tribulations beyond our control. Therefore, God allowed the Son of Man, Jesus Christ, to endure heartache and pain—and death—so we could be restored to our rightful position in Him and equipped with the authority to live fruitful lives. Jesus understands every problem we have faced. He shed His own blood so we could be set completely free.

⮜ Chapter 13 ⮞

Costly Distractions

$\mathcal{B}$y now I hope you are connecting the dots and discovering deliverance isn't usually instantaneous, but a process. It was for Jesus and it will be for us. There will be times when it appears our flesh has gained control over our spirit, but it is in these times we must press into that secret place with God, lay down our will, and trust Him to fulfill His perfect will for our lives. Jesus gives us a beautiful example in Luke's gospel.

> And He was withdrawn from them about a stone's throw, and He knelt down and prayed, saying, "Father, if it is Your will, take this cup away from Me; nevertheless not My will, but Yours, be done."

Then an angel appeared to Him from heaven, strengthening Him. (Luke 22:41–43)

Patterns

During my personal deliverance journey, I began to notice negative patterns. I was shocked when the Lord revealed to me that my own home was the place where most of my self-destructive behaviors took place. This revelation was enlightening to me. As I sought the Lord, He showed me what I needed to do, and I obeyed His promptings. I anointed my home with oil and prayed over every room. I consecrated my home to the Lord and created an atmosphere full of the Lord's presence.

I did practical things too. I kept my home clean and smelling fresh. I purchased beautiful, uplifting paintings and hung them on the walls, and I burned candles with lovely scents. It was imperative my home represented a positive environment. After I finished cleaning my house, the Lord revealed to me that He wanted to do some housecleaning of His own in my soul.

Blame Game

A toxic habit most of us discover on our deliverance journey is playing the blame game. This is not a new tactic of the enemy. Adam used it in the Garden of Eden.

Then the man said, "The woman whom You gave *to be* with me, she gave me of the tree, and I ate." (Genesis 3:12)

If we are earnest about being set free, we must recognize our unhealthy patterns and not enter the arena of blaming others. We should take full responsibility for our actions. This is extremely important because deliverance cannot and will not come until we acknowledge we have a problem and have been a willing participant.

We must be discerning and look for patterns or connections between things. We will begin to notice the biggest cause for the transgression is costly distractions.

Merriam-Webster's dictionary defines a *distraction* as "the act of distracting or the state of being distracted: especially mental confusion." *Distracted* is defined as "mentally confused, troubled, or remote."

Most of us have started a project we didn't finish. We may have started college but dropped out. Or it could be something as simple as cleaning out a closet. For some reason we were sidetracked and never finished. We can come up with many excuses why we didn't complete a task, but there is one common denominator—distractions. These interruptions can be good, bad, or indifferent, but most of the time they will keep us from accomplishing our goal.

You may be asking, "How does a distraction tie into maintaining my deliverance?" I'm glad you asked. Let me share what I have learned.

If God delivers you from alcohol, is it wise to accompany your friend to a bar? Absolutely not! If you go to a tavern, the entire time your friend is attempting to have a conversation, you would be distracted by all the liquor bottles calling your name. We shouldn't place ourselves in temptation. Most of the time, we will stumble right back into the pit the Lord is trying to deliver us from.

Pride cloaks itself in many disguises. One of the worst things we can do is to fool ourselves into thinking we no longer have to stay low at the Lord's feet. Humility always has and always will get God's attention. We must faithfully exercise a humble and contrite spirit before God and ask Him to purify our heart and soul of anything that displeases Him. Remember what His Word teaches—He resists the proud but gives grace to the humble (James 4:6).

Let us never forget that the enemy of our souls will come back to test us to see if we are delivered or not. When he finds us in a weakened sinful state, he comes back seven times stronger, so we must live close to Jesus.

> "When an unclean spirit goes out of a man, he goes through dry places, seeking rest; and finding none, he says, 'I will return to my house from which I came.' And when he comes, he finds it swept and put in order. Then he goes and takes with him seven other spirits more wicked than himself, and they enter and dwell there; and the last state of that man is worse than the first." (Luke 11:24–26)

When we have been delivered from a sinful habit, whether drugs, alcohol, pornography, gambling, lying, or any other evil act, we must refrain from putting ourselves in situations that could cause us to fall. We may have to move to a different town, sever friendships, or stop watching a particular favorite television show.

Identify

We must identify people, places, or things that are trigger points and cause us to backslide. We have to strategize how we will respond when faced with tempting distractions.

If we are wise, we will eliminate most of them, but some may be especially difficult to ignore. In those cases, we must be mentally prepared and have a game plan in place.

Take a few minutes to write down some of the distractions you face on the lines below. You can use this as a guide when developing an action plan to combat them.

_____

_____

_____

_____

_____

_____

_____

_____

_____

_____

Chapter 14

POWER IN WORSHIP

*I*n the previous chapter I spoke a little about spotting negative patterns that hinder our deliverance. In this chapter I would like to share about some positive patterns we can implement in our life that will help us experience a mighty deliverance.

As believers, we need to learn the art of true worship. God inhabits the praises of His children, and the enemy cannot stand the Lord's presence. That's why the Bible teaches us that in His presence is fullness of joy. We also are familiar with the scripture that teaches us that the joy of the Lord is our strength. Saints, it's time to worship the Lord. Let our deliverance begin.

But the hour is coming, and now is, when the true worshippers will worship the Father in spirit and truth; for the Father is seeking such to worship Him. (John 4:23)

In this passage, Jesus was talking to a divorced woman with questionable character. Two thousand years ago they stood beside a well in Samaria where He shared this powerful secret with her—His father was seeking people to be his worshippers. I think we need to return to the well of Living Water and let Jesus speak those words to us.

Worship plays a critical part in the lives of Christians. We were created to worship God and give Him praise in all things. One of the challenges many of us face is not knowing how to properly worship God. Many times we think worship only involves lifting our hands toward heaven and thanking God for everything He has done, but how do we live when the music fades? Do we find ourselves complaining about our circumstances when the worship service is over? This shouldn't be. Worship is a lifestyle, not just an emotional church service. Because of these misconceptions, I believe many people have not received breakthroughs in certain areas of their lives.

A Disciplined Life

When we become earnest about our deliverance, the Master Teacher enrolls us in His training school. We are soldiers of the cross. The Holy Spirit holds us to a higher standard. We can't just meander through life with a lackadaisical attitude. We must exercise some discipline. There are practical steps that can help us along the way. Simple little tweaks in our habits can enhance our lives. Something as simple as being on time for the worship service can build more character in our soul.

When I started getting serious about my deliverance, being prompt to church was at the top of my list. I knew if I didn't cry out and touch the Lord during the worship service, I would be lacking in spiritual strength the rest of the week. Our time of worship should focus on giving God praise just for who He is. We shouldn't be consumed with our problems and our lack. We must turn our eyes on Jesus and off of ourselves.

Counseling Session

During a session with my counselor, she stressed I would experience true worship when I concentrated on only God and not myself. I remember thinking, *This woman is nuts!* I was offended when she told me I wasn't worshipping God the right way. She challenged me to read books on prayer and worship, even instructed me to ask God for divine wisdom in this area. Soon afterward, I found myself pondering her advice. *How can I focus primarily on God and not my situation when my heart is bleeding? Doesn't God want me to let Him know when my heart is heavy and I need Him to intervene in my situation?*

My counselor created a worship CD for me and encouraged me to listen to it daily while meditating on the words. This was extremely hard for me because these songs of worship evoked emotions buried deep down in my soul. I recall the lyrics to one song that especially ministered to me: "Deliver me from the enemy within me." Just visiting the place of pain made me call on the name of Jesus. During these sacred visits from heaven, I felt myself connecting with the Lord on a deeper level. I knew He was setting up His kingdom and defeating the enemy on the inside of me.

> Neither shall they say, Lo here! or, lo there! for, behold, the kingdom of God is within you. (Luke 17:21 KJV)

Although every visit of the Holy Spirit was filled with tears and crying, I was confident God was with me during the entire process. Worship allowed me to hear His voice more clearly. God constantly reminded me how beautiful and precious I was to Him. He whispered secrets to me. "I am going to use you for My honor and glory. You are going to help others be set free."

Kirk Franklin's worship CD changed my life. Every time I turned it on, my spirit soared, except when I heard him sing "Smile." I usually skipped to the next song because the lyrics declared me beautiful and free, but I didn't see myself whole and complete. I felt completely opposite, but I longed for the day I would be able to sing the words with joy, freedom, and confidence.

A few months later that day came. I was in my car and "Smile" came on our local radio station. As I sang it with all my heart, tears streamed down my face. I experienced complete freedom in my soul. I couldn't help but "smile" and thank God I was finally at a good place physically, spiritually, and emotionally.

Don't Underestimate the Power of Worship

God has provided His Church with an arsenal of weapons that look foolish to the world, but if we will implement and use them in our lives, victory will come.

But God chose the foolish things of the world to shame the wise; God chose the weak things of the world to shame the strong. (1 Corinthians 1:27 NIV)

The Bible makes several references to God's people worshipping Him in the beauty of His holiness. David was a worshiper. Despite all he went through and the mistakes he made, he purposed in his heart to continually give God the praise. I believe his sincere spirit of worship is what made him a man after God's own heart.

So I will sing praise to Your name forever, That I may daily perform my vows. (Psalm 61:8)

Ascribe to the LORD the glory due his name; worship the LORD in the splendor of his holiness. (Psalm 29:2 NIV)

Let us go into His tabernacle; Let us worship at His footstool. (Psalm 132:7)

No matter what challenges we may be facing, we must respond like David and worship God with all our heart. Worship brings us into the Lord's glorious presence and is the key to victory.

When something is worshiped, it is respected. Respecting the fact God created us to love and walk in complete obedience to His Word is a good place to start. Settle this biblical truth in your heart. God has called you to worship Him.

Digging Deeper

According to *Strong's Exhaustive Concordance*, the

word *worship* is derived from the Greek word *proskuneo*, which means "to crouch, to bow down in homage, to adore lovingly." All the different methods of worship have this common purpose in mind: worshipping God by having a willingness to submit to His purpose and will for our life. It is when we choose God's will above our own. The total surrendering of our wills and accepting the truth that God is sovereign and comparable to none.

Worship allows us to know God intimately and serves as a reminder that we live for something greater than ourselves. Worship is must in our lives. We can't function without it. We don't necessarily need to be in a church service to give God praise. We can drive in our car and begin to lift up His name and thank Him for his goodness and mercy. Whenever we have a few minutes, we can use them to worship God. We can exalt Him and magnify His mighty name

Jehovah-Jireh: Our Provider

Jehovah-Nissi: Our Banner and Victory

Jehovah-M'Kaddesh: Our Sanctifier

Jehovah-Baal-perazim: Our Breakthrough

Jehovah-Shalom: Our Peace

Jehovah-Rapha: Our Healer

Coming to a full understanding of worship will not only deepen our relationship with God, but it will also lead us to deliverance. We must be wise and understand the adversary will make every effort to keep us from spending time in the presence of God. He knows something supernatural takes place in the spirit when we worship God. When we lift Him up and exalt Him for who He is and not what He can do for us, miracles will take place. God even provides safety in worship.

He who dwells in the secret place of the Most High
Shall abide under the shadow of the Almighty.
(Psalm 91:1 KJV)

When we are dwelling in this secret place, our
relationship with God becomes stronger. It is in this place
that intimacy with our heavenly Father is birthed. Then He
is able to impregnate us with His vision for our lives. There is
liberty, victory, and deliverance in the Lord's presence.

Now the Lord is the Spirit; and where the Spirit of
the Lord *is*, there *is* liberty. (2 Corinthians 3:17)

Sometimes I wonder if we really understand what this
Scripture is saying. To me it is plain and simple—anything
contrary to the Word of God can't remain in the life of
believers when the Spirit of the Lord abides in them.

This should be a favorite foundational scripture we can
stand on throughout our deliverance process. When we are
in His presence, there is anointing to set the captives free.

When we get to the place where the Spirit of God resides,
we will be free from depression, oppression, low self-esteem,
and other forms of bondage.

Practice His Presence

Oh, dear children of God, we don't have to wait for a
church service to be in His presence. We can practice His
presence wherever we are. When we learn the art of creating
an environment conducive for His Spirit, the chains of
darkness will fall off us.

It is imperative we understand God isn't the source of
any of our pain. But we also need to know He never wastes our
hurts. He is able to use our experiences to perfect and cleanse

us from all unrighteousness. Keep in mind, our decision to worship God during these experiences is crucial to the outcome of our situation. God desires to perfect everything that concerns us.

We may be facing fierce attacks from the enemy, but we have the weapon of praise and worship to completely change the atmosphere where we are. God always shows up in an atmosphere permeated with worship. The demons can't stand it, but God gets excited when we lift up His name.

Do you remember the familiar story about Paul and Silas in the New Testament? They were beaten and thrown in jail for preaching the gospel. God was in heaven minding His business, but then He heard His faithful servants singing hymns and spiritual songs in the darkest hour of their lives. Even though their situation looked bleak, Paul and Silas still worshipped. Their praises moved the Father. Heaven came to earth and the shackles fell off and prison doors were miraculously opened. When we worship God, we position ourselves in a supernatural realm. All things become possible. Something shifts in heaven and our deliverance is made available to us.

Prayer

Father, Your Word says Your people perish for a lack of knowledge. I thank You for bringing clarification in this area of worship to me. Lord, teach me how to worship You in Spirit and in Truth. From this moment forward I purpose in my heart to apply what You have taught me. Amen.

☞ Chapter 15 ☜

PREPARING FOR DELIVERANCE

*W*e have arrived at a good spiritual place when we recognize the need for deliverance in areas of our life. We are at a redefining moment in our lives. No longer do we have to be tormented by past mistakes. We can experience and walk in the freedom only Christ can give.

I will present several steps in this chapter that must be taken to be delivered. Carefully meditate and complete each step. Listen as God speaks to your heart. The most difficult part, getting to the root of your problems, is over. Now you can effectively take authority over the strongman and defeat him once and for all. The battle has already been won for you by Jesus's death and resurrection. Oh, dear friend, He paid a great price for us to be free. Let's take advantage of everything He has provided for us.

Born Again

Let's review a few steps. First, please take inventory of your spiritual condition. Ask yourself, "Has there been a time in my life when I accepted Jesus Christ into my heart and life?"

Before He can rule on the throne of our hearts, He must be invited in. The Bible makes this marvelous promise:

> If you confess with your mouth the Lord Jesus and believe in your heart that God has raised Him from the dead, you will be saved. (Romans 10:9)

If you feel the least bit unsure you are saved or if you need to rededicate your life to Christ, let's settle it once and for all. Just sincerely pray this prayer aloud:

> *Father, I come before you right now thanking You for health, life, and strength. I ask You to forgive my sins and come live within my heart. I confess Jesus Christ is Lord and believe He died and was raised from the dead for my complete deliverance. I believe with all my heart that I am saved from destruction and rejoice that my name has been written in the Lamb's Book of Life. Thank You that I am now accepted into Your fold. Amen.*

Through the Years

Through the years, I have researched and read numerous books on deliverance. My library is filled with books on this topic. I had an insatiable hunger to learn what other great men and woman of God were teaching on this subject. I was determined to be free.

While embarking on this journey, I discovered *They Shall Expel Demons* by Derek Prince, one of the greatest Bible teachers in the body of Christ. Reverend Prince did an excellent job of explaining the process of deliverance, restoration, and healing. The following steps are a combination of Reverend Prince's suggestions and mine, inspired by the Holy Spirit.

Eight Steps through Deliverance to Freedom in Christ

✓ 1—Personally affirm your faith in Christ.
✓ 2—Confess any known sin.
✓ 3—Repent and make restitution for all sins.
✓ 4—Forgive all others.
✓ 5—Denounce any involvement with the occult and all false religions.
✓ 6—Prepare to be released from every curse over your life.
✓ 7—Take your stand with God.
✓ 8—Expel.

1—Personally affirm your faith in Christ.

Your words must consistently line up with the Word of God. Be observant and sensitive to what you are confessing with your mouth. This is imperative for walking in victory. The Bible declares in Hebrews 3:1, "Jesus is the High Priest of our confession." If He is the High Priest of our confession, what He says should be the only thing articulated with our mouth. We shouldn't make negative statements about ourselves. The enemy's goal is to get our confession to be contrary to the Word of God. We must speak truth and life.

Whenever we travel to different parts of the country, the first thing we notice is usually people's accents. We can identify where they come from by the way they talk. I believe heaven has an accent all its own fluently spoken around God's throne. The Bible gives us a peek behind the scenes of heaven. There is a great deal of praise and thanksgiving taking place. As believers, we should imitate those faithful ones. Our lips should speak forth His goodness. If our words and lives demonstrate our faith, revival fires will spread through our families, neighborhoods, churches, and country. Today we must let the whole world know through our speech and actions that Jesus died for them.

2—Confess any known sin.

> If we confess our sins, He is faithful and just to forgive us our sins and to cleanse us from all unrighteousness. (1 John 1:9 KJV)

You may wonder why we have to confess our sins when God already knows what we did. First, because the Bible tells us this is the only way our sins are forgiven. Second, when we confess our sins, we take ownership them and then God can extend forgiveness to us.

God wants us to come to him and share our hearts, including our faults and shortcomings. Even though the Bible also teaches we are to confess our sins one to another, God never wants us to think the power lies within our peers. God is the ultimate Judge and He forgives us of our trespasses. His Word is true. He is faithful and just to cleanse us of all unrighteousness.

3—Repent and make restitution for all sins.

In addition to confessing our sins, it is important that we thoroughly repent and make restitution for our sins.

> He who covers sins will not prosper, but whoever confesses and forsakes them will have mercy. (Proverbs 28:13)

There may be some sins we are unable to make right. I heard of a man who was a thief. He stole money from several businesses before he was saved. After he gave his heart to the Lord, he saw his need to make restitution. He wrote a letter to every business he had stolen from and repaid his debt, plus a little extra. There were two businesses that had shut down. He made every attempt to pay back what he had stolen, but the owners had since passed away. One night in prayer he asked the Lord what he should do. The Holy Spirit led him to write a check and place it in the offering plate at his church. He immediately obeyed. A great weight was lifted when he made restitution. I cannot express enough how important it is to take responsibility for our actions. These steps must come from the heart or this process will be in vain.

4—Forgive all other people.

This teaching is very difficult for most people. In the beginning I struggled with forgiveness too. I thought certain things were unforgiveable, especially when people didn't take responsibility for their offense. I quickly realized the only person I was hurting was me. Forgiveness is a mandatory prerequisite for receiving personal forgiveness from God. If we want to live in freedom, we must forgive. If we don't,

God cannot forgive us. Jesus established this nonnegotiable spiritual law.

> "And whenever you stand praying, if you have anything against anyone, forgive him, that your Father in heaven may also forgive you your trespasses. But if you do not forgive, neither will your Father in heaven forgive your trespasses." (Mark 11:25-26)

This passage clearly states we must forgive others if we want to be forgiven. The need to do this is not contingent on anything. It's a matter of fact. The Word of God doesn't show partiality. Rape, murder, or adultery. It doesn't matter. God calls us to forgive the person from our hearts. When unforgiveness festers in our hearts, we have allowed the enemy to build a makeshift prison in our minds.

One way you can determine if you have failed to forgive someone: Examine your heart for resentment. In most cases, when you discover resentment, unforgiveness is also present.

Webster defines *resentment* as "a feeling of indignant displeasure or persistent ill will at something regarding as wrong, insult, or injury." We must ask the Lord to search our heart for areas we have not forgiven, and He will reveal them to us. Once He does, it is our responsibility to forgive from our hearts. When we do, God is able to heal our wounds.

If we desire for God to forgive us of our sins, we must allow Him to forgive others for their wrong doing. God loves each of us equally. He doesn't play favorites with His children. Forgiveness is ultimately for us. When we release people, painful situations, and the hurt they may have caused, we are positioned to receive blessings from God.

Forgiving others who have wounded us allows healing to manifest not only emotionally but physically in our life. I know of believers who received a complete mental and physical healing when they could let go and let God have His way. I experienced my own physical touch from the Lord after I extended forgiveness to certain individuals who hurt me. The Lupus I had been diagnosed with stayed in remission. Overall, I felt better. Rejuvenation replaced fatigue and depression. I experienced joy. I have determined I will not allow unforgiveness to cause me to forfeit the abundant life ever again.

5—Denounce any involvement with the occult and all false religions.

The Word of God teaches there are many spirits in this world. Many times, if we have experienced deep hurt and pain, we go on a search for the "truth." The enemy of our souls presents "false truths" that do not line up with God's Word. Hungry souls explore strange religions and unknowingly open doors, giving evil spirits access to our life. Satan devises plans and schemes to divert our attention from God to deceptive systems such as horoscopes, tarot cards, fortune telling, Ouija Boards, and other dark practices.

My Experience

When I was a little girl, I signed up to be a Brownie, a branch of the Girl Scouts for five- to nine-year-old girls. One October we had a Halloween block party. Every house on the street participated by decorating their houses with a spooky theme. Some were fortune tellers and others were haunted houses. I entered one of the fortune teller houses. A woman asked me to sit down and place my hands in her hands with my palms facing up. Directly in front of her was a crystal ball. She rubbed the ball and my hands simultaneously for a few minutes.

"You will be fast and hot!" Her eyes seemed to see through me. "You will run after boys and get into a lot of trouble."

I stared straight ahead. Although I didn't understand what she was saying, I did feel uneasy. I knew what she was telling me was wrong.

Years later when I was in middle school, I was introduced to Ouija boards. My childhood friend and I lied to her mother. We made some story up about needing a Ouija board to complete a science project. Her mother took us to Toy R Us and she purchased the board. That evening we were in my friend's bedroom anticipating whether or not we should play. We read the instructions and it explained we needed to place both hands on the pointer and ask the spirits questions.

We were laughing, but deep down we were nervous. We followed the directions, but nothing seemed to be happening. The pointer wasn't moving. We started giggling and chanting, "Come out, come out, wherever you are." Eventually, the pointer started moving by itself. We were in complete shock. My friend began asking questions about her future and the pointer would move to different letters on the board, actively spelling out the answer. I remember her asking the spirits the age she was going to get pregnant. The spirit responded age seventeen. I asked the board its name. It spelled out RACHI. I didn't know what or who that was. My friend yanked her hands back and gasped, "Rachi is my cousin's dead mother!"

"Are you serious?"

"Yes! She died a couple years ago," my friend shot back.

My heart sank. I removed my hands from the pointer and whispered a quick prayer. I shared with my friend how bad and evil the Ouija board was. "We shouldn't play it anymore."

Fear gripped my heart as the pointer spelled profane language and then spelled out my name. We decided to throw the board in the garbage can.

Shut the Door and Keep out the Devil

One day a precious woman of God was teaching from God's Word. "When we know better, we do better."

Many times we open doors out of pure ignorance, but when we gain knowledge in these areas, we must immediately repent and rebuke demonic spirits. They have no legal ground to be in our lives when we have applied the blood of the Lamb over our hearts. The only way they can enter is if we give them access. Let's shut the door and keep out the devil!

Queen Nefertiti Charm

I remember another incident that occurred when I was in my last year of college. A lady brought her eight-month-old baby to class with her every week. She seemed so determined to get her degree and I admired her tenacity. One evening after class, we had an interesting conversation about God and religion. I can't recall the details, but I do remember her telling me she was a pastor, and I felt very comfortable sharing with her about some of the challenges I was facing. She listened intently and then explained how we give access to the enemy when we live in sin. Her words ministered to my hungry soul. She noticed a Queen Nefertiti charm on my

115

necklace and asked, "Are you familiar with the story about the children of Israel and Egypt?"

"Kind of."

She explained, "God told the children of Israel to leave and take no foreign gods with them. Do you know why?"

Once again, I shook my head. "No."

"Evil spirits can attach themselves to things, and we must be careful what we wear and bring in our home."

I was shocked. Never in my life had I heard teaching like this. After I thanked her for her wisdom and discernment, I immediately took the charm off and threw it in the garbage. As I drove home, I prayed and asked God to continue to teach me so I wouldn't be ignorant of the enemy's devices. When I arrived home, I went into the bedroom and spotted the charm I had thrown away a few minutes earlier lying on my dresser. I was in utter disbelief—and I was petrified! I prayed against the spirit of fear and threw the charm in the garbage. I never saw it again.

If we open doors to the occult, we have given the enemy legal ground to bring harm, torment, sickness, disease, lack, and every other negative curse to our life. We may do things in ignorance. I never dreamed a charm could be so devilish.

People visit psychics and play tarot cards out of ignorance. We all have done some things in our lives not realizing the consequences attached to it. That's why it is important we recognize and denounce all involvement with the occult. We must obey in word and deed. We speak it and then we put actions to our words. We remove from our possession anything that links us to the occult. People will be surprised at how many subtle things such as books, mugs, souvenirs, charms, or art are attached to the occult. We must be wise and discerning.

The Bible is gives us an example of a wonderful way to dispose of occult paraphernalia—burn them. This is how the Christians in Ephesus responded when they realized their occult scrolls linked them to the power of demons.

> A number who had practiced sorcery brought their scrolls together and burned them publicly. When they calculated the value of the scrolls, the total came to fifty thousand drachmas. In this way the word of the Lord spread widely and grew in power. (Acts 19:19–20 NIV)

We don't have to walk in fear because as children of God we have victory over the devil, but this is a step that must be taken to ensure complete deliverance.

6—Prepare to be released from every curse on your life.

For years the word *curse* has been taboo in the Church. It appears to have a negative connotation, but a curse is nothing for the Body of Christ to fear because God has already given us the power and authority to break every curse over our life and the lives of others.

In Deuteronomy 28, the Bible clearly spells out the blessings we are entitled to receive if we obey God's commandments. However, we tend to stop reading after the blessings are mentioned. Look further down in the chapter to find several verses pertaining to curses that result from disobedience, personal or generational. Although we are under the dispensation of grace, if we are not careful, we can open ourselves to curses.

According to Webster's dictionary a *curse* is defined as "a cause of great harm or misfortune." It is important we recognize when a curse is in operation so we can effectively pray to destroy it.

Here is a list of several common problems indicating a curse could be at work:

- ✓ Severe depression, anxiety, or nervous breakdown
- ✓ Infertility, repeated miscarriages and other female reproductive problems
- ✓ Severe marriage problems, separation, and divorce
- ✓ Constant poverty and financial instability
- ✓ Repeated accidents
- ✓ Suicide or untimely or premature death

Please don't misunderstand this list. Just because you are experiencing some of these things does not necessarily mean you are under a curse. Pray and ask God to reveal to you any area of your life linked to a curse. Many of the things we experienced in our life is the result of a curse. It doesn't have to be something you did. The Bible teaches about the sins our ancestors having a direct effect on us, but the good news is we can be free in Jesus Christ.

> Christ redeemed us from the curse of the law by becoming a curse for us, for it is written: "Cursed is everyone who is hung on a pole." He redeemed us in order that the blessing given to Abraham might come to the Gentiles through Christ Jesus, so that by faith we might receive the promise of the Spirit. (Galatians 3:13–14 NIV)

You can be free today! Comb through this list and

identify which things pertain to you. You may even notice patterns in your life producing negative results. Add this to your list as well. When the Holy Spirit deals with you about certain areas, write it down. Pray over what He shows you.

7—Take your stand with God.

When we know God intimately and become familiar with His Word, we can confidently take our stand. We will never be able to take our stand with God if we don't know what He stands for. Most of our questions will be answered if we just spend time in His presence and devour His Word. There is impartation as we read the Bible. His Holy Spirit speaks to us and reveals divine truths. One of the most triumphant truths is this—no one is greater than our God. No demon in hell can defeat Him. We are more than conquerors.

> What, then, shall we say in response to these things? If God is for us, who can be against us? (Romans 8:31 NIV)

Oh Church, I've read the back of the Book and we win! God is on our side. Let's dedicate and consecrate our entire life to Him. He will cause us to have victory along every line.

8—Expel.

This step is difficult to write because I want to make sure it is written with clarity and understanding. The enemy will definitely attempt to bring fear and intimidation during this part of the deliverance process. There is no need to fear because God has given us the power and authority to trample over every unclean thing.

As I stated in the previous chapter, when people are engaged in habitual sin, doors will open in their life that gives the enemy control. For example, when a person watches pornography and masturbates, a spirit of perversion enters. I am not saying the person is demon-possessed, but a door has been opened to allow spirits to come in, tormenting and oppressing that soul. Pornography is more addictive than meth. Those bound by this dark addiction find themselves increasing the amount of time they have to watch porn. They are never satisfied. Let me add, the spirit of perversion includes not only pornography. Incest, adultery, fornication, and homosexuality are just a few sins that fall into this category as well.

After we open a door to the enemy, we must backtrack. Slam the door shut and then cast out the wicked one. When a demonic spirit is expelled, it must have an exit. *Expel* means "to push or drive something out with force." So after you have said your prayer for deliverance and concluded with "Amen," begin to expel. This is a decision of your will, followed by an action of your muscles.

When I reached this step during my deliverance process, I began coughing and throwing up. I just felt sick to my stomach. For a few days afterward, my mouth filled with saliva, which caused the need to spit. The Holy Spirit has different outward manifestations to drive out darkness. Everyone's experiences will be different.

There was a young minister who struggled with severe depression. Shadows would come over him, and he struggled to get up and preach during those oppressive days. He was a man who was faithful in his devotional life, spending much time in Bible study and prayer. One day the

Holy Spirit whispered to his soul, "I want to make you a vessel of my glory!"

He wept before the Lord because he knew his life did not glorify God with his moody disposition. He began to praise the Lord aloud. The Holy Spirit shook him from the top of his head to the soles of his feet. After several minutes the shaking stopped and the Lord revealed to him what was taking place. God was driving the darkness from his body. For years he had given into his dark moods. They had become imbedded in his soul. Even though he was born again, the Holy Spirit did a deeper work and completely freed him of his former bondages.

There will be manifestations as the Holy Spirit is being poured out. Some people sigh or yawn. Others may sob, groan, cough, scream, or roar. Just yield your body to the Holy Spirit and let Him do His work to give you a mighty deliverance.

⁓ Chapter 16 ⁓

A PRAYER FOR DELIVERANCE

*T*ake a deep breath and smile. Half the battle is over. When you finish with the eight steps, you have reached the point where you can claim and receive your deliverance through faith and effective prayer. This chapter will provide an outline to serve as a prayer guide. Keep in mind, this is just an outline. Feel free to pray as the Holy Spirit leads. I just want to supply you with some prayer ideas that may inspire you as you continue your deliverance process.

Jesus made it clear that certain victories are won only through prayer combined with fasting. I found it very helpful to fast before taking part in the deliverance prayer portion of this chapter. There are plenty of books on the power of prayer and fasting. I encourage you to do a Bible study on this subject so you can gain further knowledge and have a deeper understanding.

> So He said to them, "This kind can come out by nothing but prayer and fasting." (Mark 9:29)

Take your time with each step. God does not look at time the same way we do. One thousand years is a day to Him. He is never in a rush and we shouldn't be either. Allow the Holy Spirit to speak to your heart and deal with you during the deliverance process. I've provided a place for you to jot down your feelings and thoughts about each prayer. When you are asked to forgive others, write their names in the blanks so you can include them in your prayer.

1. **Personally affirm your faith in Christ.**

   Jesus Christ, I believe with all my heart that you are the Son of God and the only path to God. You died on the Cross specifically for me and rose again so I could be forgiven of my sins and receive eternal life.

2. **Confess any known sin.**

   Father God, I openly confess all my sins before you. I confess . . . _____

   _____

   _____

   _____

3. **Repent of all sins.**

   I repent of all my sins and deliberately make a decision to turn away from them and turn to You, Lord, for strength, mercy, and forgiveness. Father, forgive me for . . . _____

_____

_____

_____

_____

_____

4.   **Forgive all other people.**

Lord, I choose to forgive all those individuals who
have hurt, abused, and misused me in any way. I
choose to no longer be bitter or angry. I will no
longer harbor resentment in my heart. Specifically,
I forgive . . . _____

_____

_____

_____

_____

5.   **Denounce any involvement with the occult and
any other false religion.**

I sever all contact I ever had with the occult any other
false religion. Particularly, I commit myself to get
rid of all objects associated with the occult or false
religion._____

_____

_____

_____

6.   **Prepare to be released from every curse over
your life.**

Father God, I thank You for allowing Jesus Christ to

die and be resurrected from the dead because that qualified me for redemption. So now Father, I ask you to release and set me free to receive the deliverance I need. _____

_____
_____
_____

7. **Take your stand with God.**

Lord, I take my stand with You. I come against all satanic powers. I submit willingly to You and Your will for my life and I resist the devil In Jesus' name. Amen.

List anything that may hinder you from going all out for Jesus. _____

_____
_____
_____
_____

8. **Expel.**

Now speak directly to any demons or evil spirits that have control over you. Insist they go from you now in the precious name of Jesus. I expel you!

Write down ways God has delivered you. _____

_____
_____
_____
_____
_____

⇜ Chapter 17 ⇝

HOW TO KEEP YOUR DELIVERANCE

$\mathcal{B}$elievers should be the happiest people on the planet, especially those who have experienced the delivering power of the Holy Spirit. God's praises should flow from their lips and spill out of their lives.

The enemy is not at all happy with us when we get serious about our deliverance. He will do everything in his power to make us his prisoner again. As I have mentioned in a previous chapter, once demonic spirits have been released, they will definitely return, hoping to find an entrance. We must make every effort to keep our lives full of the Holy Spirit so there is no room for the wicked one.

When the enemy receives access in our lives, he immediately wraps invisible chains around our souls, creating strongholds and giving an illusion they are permanent. He whispers lies in our ears: "This is who you really are. You can't change. Your father had the same problem. There is no hope!"

Satan is a liar. He wants you to live a pauper's existence, but God's Word declares you are a child of the King. Jesus has set you free by the power of His precious blood.

Let's determine to not give the enemy an inch! Now that he has been driven out, we must delve into the Bible and discover who we are in Christ. This will boost our confidence, renew our spiritual man, and maintain safeguards.

Here are some fundamental biblical principles to help us rebuild our lives and keep our faith vibrant and fresh.

- **Live by God's Word.**

  But He answered and said, "It is written, 'Man shall not live by bread alone, but by every word that proceeds from the mouth of God.'" (Matthew 4:4)

  The only way we will know what proceeds out of the mouth of God is studying His Word. Afterward we must apply it in every area of our life. God's Word must always be the final authority in our life.

- **Put off our old man and put on the garment of praise.**

  Put off, concerning your former conduct, the old man which grows corrupt according to the deceitful lusts, and be renewed in the spirit of your mind, and that you put on the new man which was created according to God, in true righteousness and holiness. (Ephesians 4:22–24)

To console those who mourn in Zion, To give them beauty for ashes, The oil of joy for mourning, The garment of praise for the spirit of heaviness; That they may be called trees of righteousness, The planting of the LORD, that He may be glorified." (Isaiah 61:3)

God has given us a new wardrobe. We don't have to dress in the dreary garments we used to wear. Before my deliverance I was bound up in my old grave clothes, but Jesus said, "Loose her and let her go." No longer was I to carry around that spirit of heaviness, but He gave me the garment of praise. When the enemy tries to tempt me to wear my old tattered garments of depression, I put on my new outfit of praise. It is not long before the devil has to flee. He can't stand the Lord's presence, but we survive and thrive there.

As we cultivate an attitude of gratitude, our lives are changed forever. No longer will we be "grumbly hateful." Instead we are "humbly grateful." Our new lifestyle of praise and thanksgiving is more contagious than chicken pox. Soon people will be saying, "I want what she has."

Praise will help us soar in every valley. Regardless of what we experience or feel, praise is the answer. Each time we open our mouth and give God praise, the atmosphere must line up to what we have declared out of our mouth. Don't neglect your garment of praise.

- **Come under discipline.**

  For the Spirit God gave us does not make us timid, but gives us power, love and self-discipline. (2 Timothy 1:7 NIV)

Until we learn to walk in the Spirit and to use the art of self- control, our lives will be ineffective. When we commune with the Father on a daily basis, we learn about His attributes and begin to desire them for ourselves. Our mind will be renewed and our actions will line up with the Word of God. Communing with the Lord allows the Holy Spirit to transform us, bringing our emotions, desires, and appetites under control. We will reflect our Father. He will stamp His image on our hearts.

- **Be filled with the Holy Spirit.**

  Do not get drunk on wine, which leads to debauchery. Instead, be filled with the Spirit, speaking to one another with psalms, hymns, and songs from the Spirit. Sing and make music from your heart to the Lord, always giving thanks to God the Father for everything, in the name of our Lord Jesus Christ. (Ephesians 5:18–29 NIV)

  The infilling of the Holy Spirit gives us power to live right. He enables us to live victoriously and be more than conquerors for Him.

- **Develop godly friendships.**

  Do not be misled: "Bad company corrupts good character." (1 Corinthians 15:33 NIV)

  We must develop friendships in the Lord and surround ourselves with other believers. These relationships will provide accountability and play a vital role in the success of our deliverance. Because of the powerful influences people hold in our lives, we must use wisdom in choosing who we associate with. By no means, however, should we be judgmental with Pharisaic attitudes. We should extend God's love to all people, but if we are going to walk in the freedom Christ has for us, we must decide to live upright before the Lord and present ourselves in a Christlike manner. We must associate with individuals who have similar desires.

- **Put on the whole armor of God.**

  Therefore put on the full armor of God, so that when the day of evil comes, you may be able to stand your ground, and after you have done everything, to stand. (Ephesians 6:13 NIV)

  We are in a war! The enemy is out to kill, steal, and destroy our lives. He shows no mercy and is uninterested in our feelings. His main focus is to wreak havoc in our life any way he can, but we have a heavenly Father! He loves us and has a divine destiny for us to fulfill. We are to live in total and complete victory in every area of our lives. He has provided an arsenal of weapons for every soldier of the Cross. We can defeat the enemy with them.

- **Wear the girdle of truth.**

  Stand firm then, with the belt of truth buckled around your waist. (Ephesians 6:14 NIV)

  A tight-fitting girdle holds everything together. This is a good illustration of how the belt of truth holds our life together in proper perspective and maintains integrity.

  In biblical times men usually wore loose clothing that hung down below their knees. Before under-

taking any strenuous activity, they would father
up their loose garment above their knees and fasten it with a belt around the waist. Likewise, we
must gather up and fasten out of the way anything
that would impede your freedom to follow Jesus.
The "belt" that enables you to do this is God's
Word, applied in a very plain and practical way.
You must become totally sincere and open and put
aside every form of dishonesty or hypocrisy. You
must love the truth. (Prince, 1998)

- **Keep the breastplate of righteousness in place.**

  Stand firm then, with the breastplate of righteousness in place. (Ephesians 6:13 NIV)

The breastplate protects the most important and critical
area on our body—our heart.

  Guard your heart above all else, for it determines
  the course of your life. (Proverbs 4:23 NLT)

We must protect our heart and not allow it to be
contaminated by the world but preserve it with the
righteousness of Christ dwelling in our heart and manifesting
through our daily life.

- **Wear the shoes of the preparation of the gospel
  of peace.**

  And with your feet fitted with the readiness that
  comes from the gospel of peace. (Ephesians 6:15
  NIV)

Wearing shoes allows us to be mobile. Footwear shields our feet from injuries we could receive if we walk around barefooted. Wearing the shoes of the preparation of the gospel of peace encourages us that God will direct every step if we allow Him to. He will position us right where we need to be to share the gospel of Jesus Christ. He has also given us a peace that strengthens our heart to know there is nothing missing or nothing broken.

- **Take up the shield of faith.**

  In addition to all this, take up the shield of faith, with which you can extinguish all the flaming arrows of the evil one. (Ephesians 6:16 NIV)

When shields were used years ago, they covered the soldier's entire body because they were so large. A shield could help him stay out of harm's way, but only if he knew how to use it properly. We must learn how to walk in faith. This principle governs our life in Christ.

- **Take the helmet of salvation.**

  Take the helmet of salvation. (Ephesians 6:17 NIV)

The enemy will do everything in his power to confuse us. He will whisper negative lies, attempting to create doubt in our mind about the promises of God.

I've often wondered about Golgotha, the place where Jesus was crucified. Scholars call it "the place of the skull." Jesus won a battle over Satan there. We too will have our Golgothas. The conflict will be in our mind. We must put on our helmet of salvation and fight against satanic assaults.

As children of God, we are entitled to the blessings of our Father. We must believe God's Word with all our heart, practice an intimate relationship with Him, and guard our heart and mind through Christ Jesus.

- **Take the sword of the Spirit, the Word of God.**

    Take the sword of the Spirit, which is the word of God. (Ephesians 6:17 NIV)

    The Word of God is the final authority! The Bible becomes a sword when we speak it with our mouth. Jesus used the Word when the enemy tempted him in the Garden of Gethsemane. Every time the enemy tries to distract us, we should follow Jesus' example and respond with the Word of God. It is our greatest defense against the enemy.

- **Use the final weapon: all prayer.**

    And pray in the Spirit on all occasions with all kinds of prayers and requests. With this in mind, be alert and always keep on praying for all the Lord's people. (Ephesians 6:18 NIV)

    Prayer has the ability to reach any height or depth in the Spirit. Prayer is the heartbeat of freedom. When we develop and mature in our prayer life, we will be unstoppable in the Spirit.

Maintenance

Maintaining deliverance is a process. To continue walking in victory and keep our deliverance, we must live our life according to biblical principles. Throughout the

New Testament are Scriptures depicting what a Christian life resembles.

Let's consecrate our heart and life afresh and anew to the Lord. Let's dedicate ourselves to prayer. Our Father is waiting to share His heart with us. He desires deep intimacy with His children.

The Bible doesn't give us a definite time we should spend in prayer, but when you truly desire to get to know someone, you will make quality time for them. We should set a time we can keep and meet the Lord there every day. He will not disappoint us.

∼ Chapter 18 ∼

BLOOD TRANSFUSION

*W*e have reached the final chapter of my book, but it's not the end of our journey. I pray you have been inspired and equipped to receive your deliverance, healing, and restoration. Don't lose sight of the end results! God is restoring your joy and hope!

> Not only so, but we also glory in our sufferings, because we know that suffering produces perseverance; perseverance, character; and character, hope. And hope does not put us to shame, because God's love has been poured out into our hearts through the Holy Spirit, who has been given to us. (Romans 5:3–5 NIV)

During this process, we need to continue allowing the Holy Spirit to guide us. We have a Father who loves us and desires to see us prosper in every area of our life. He will never leave or forsake us. We are safe when we abide in Him. He always holds His own and never embarrasses or condemns us for past mistakes. He welcomes us just as the prodigal son was welcomed back home by his father after going astray. Our Father is waiting on us. As He cradles us in His arms, the chains of bondage will snap in two. We will experience an indescribable freedom in worship. Laughter will return to our spirit. We will find ourselves smiling through all kinds of situations because we know our God is in control. Our joy and confidence will be renewed. We will see ourselves differently. If we stop and sit still long enough to get a glimpse of what God has in store for us, we will be astonished and motivated to get some things right in our life.

Our Father loves us. Our names are engraved on the palms of His hands. He desires to see us excel in every area of our lives.

See, I have engraved you on the palms of my hands. (Isaiah 49:16 NIV)

I have experienced some major challenges along my spiritual journey, but I thank God for my process of deliverance. Sometimes we can receive things too quickly and don't appreciate their full value. I needed my deliverance to manifest over a period of time because it forced me to deal with the root causes of my issues.

In the Song of Solomon 2:15, the Bible says, "It's the small foxes that spoil the vine." Sometimes, we don't realize the things we consider mediocre or minute are the very things preventing us from walking in our fullest potential. I grew weary of falling down and having to pick myself back up. God's Word teaches a higher way. We don't have to continue stumbling over our own disguise. He is able to keep us from falling. We are called to be victors not victims. He will take our messy situations in life and make them a message. He will turn our tests into tremendous testimonies.

> To him who is able to keep you from stumbling and to present you before his glorious presence without fault and with great joy. (Jude 1:24 NIV)

Looking Back

When I reminisce, I remember the many nights of crying and feeling alone. Depression, oppression, inadequacy, and a wave of unstable emotions ruled my life. One day I was up and the next day I was down. Psychiatrists would have diagnosed my mental state as bipolar, but Dr. Jesus appeared on the scene and gave me a personal invitation.

> "Come to me, all you who are weary and burdened, and I will give you rest. Take my yoke upon you and learn from me, for I am gentle and humble in heart, and you will find rest for your souls. (Matthew 11:28–29 NIV)

Dr. Jesus helped me confront the issues in my life. He pointed out the spirit of heaviness and then prescribed the antidote I needed. No longer did I mask the symptoms of my depression. Dr. Jesus eliminated my instability completely.

God Painted His Masterpiece in Red

Jesus gave me a supernatural blood transfusion. When I finally realized I couldn't defeat my issues in my own strength and surrendered all to God, I saw the manifestations of His power in my life. Jesus' blood was not shed in vain. God painted His masterpiece, the Cross, in red. When we accept Jesus into our heart and lives, we become His masterpiece, and His blood covers our sins. He gives us a supernatural blood transfusion and makes us the best version of us we could ever be. Oh, child of God, royal blood flows through your veins. You have a power source you can tap into and defeat the enemy.

Satan doesn't want you to know this information because he understands when you begin to exercise your authority, he is a defeated foe. Claim what belongs to you and know your true identity in Christ. Learn your resources! Study your weapons! There is healing in the blood of Jesus! There is deliverance in the blood of Jesus! There is restoration in the blood of Jesus! There is victory in the blood of Jesus! God has provided all you need.

Victorious Life

To live a victorious life, you must know who you are in Christ. The Bible is full of scriptures that tell how God views His creation. Make a commitment to study the Word of God daily. If you have difficulty understanding the Scriptures, read other versions of the Bible. We live in a great day. Many resources are available to help us on our spiritual journey. Don't allow the enemy to discourage you. The Holy Spirit is here on earth to lead us into all truth and make things plain for us.

Lakeisha Dixon's Book

In Lakeisha Dixon's phenomenal book, *The Victorious State of Mind*, she discusses the importance of opening our mouths and declaring something great every day. She teaches that many of us live defeated lives because of the words we speak. I highly recommend her book. It will change your life.

Below I have listed several confessions the Lord gave me. I encourage you to say them daily. Write them down and keep them in an accessible place. Confess them aloud with confidence. Positive faith confessions will bring great results. Remember, our lives are transformed by the words we speak. Be aware of what you're speaking and make sure your words speak life.

Who Am I?

Who Am I? I am the righteousness of God created for His glory.

Who Am I? I am royal priesthood, a chosen generation.

Who Am I? I am a change agent, world shaker, and monumental mover in this world.

Who Am I? I am more than a conqueror and will not be tormented by my past errors.

Who Am I? I am wonderful and beautiful in the sight of the Lord.

Who Am I? I am victorious and a winner in every situation.

Who Am I? I am an overcomer who consistently excels in all endeavors.

Who Am I? I am a joint heir with Jesus and entitled to all the many blessings of Abraham.

Who Am I? I am the apple of God's eye and He smiles upon me with every thought.

Who Am I? I am delivered and set free from the power of darkness.

Who Am I? I am called, appointed, and anointed for such a time as this.

Who Am I? I am the vehicle God uses to channel His wealth to the kingdom.

Who Am I? I am a skilled warrior prepared for battle.

Who Am I? I am portal of glory for the Lord.

Who Am I? I am replica of Jesus who walks in a greater authority.

Who Am I? I am a distribution center of love, joy, and peace.

Who Am I? I am a favor center. People are drawn to me daily.

Who Am I? I am full of potential and have been catapulted into greatness.

Who Am I? I am confident and make decisions that produce victory.

Who Am I? I am wise and the elite summons me daily for wisdom and knowledge.

Who Am I? I am unique, separate, and whole.

Who Am I? I am an executioner. I complete all assignments the Lord has given me.

Who Am I? I am valuable in the sight of men and the Lord.

Who Am I? I am a vault diamond that always has to be handled with care.

Who Am I? I am Royal Priesthood and accepted into the Beloved.

Who Am I? I am confident, bold, and well-respected.

Who Am I? I am a child of the Most High covered in righteousness.

Who Am I? I am empowered to prosper in every area of my life.

Who Am I? I am equipped with the authority of God and walk in power.

Who Am I? I am sharp, swift, and capable of thriving in any atmosphere.

Who Am I? I am the apple of God's eye.

Who Am I? I am important and my opinion matters.

Who Am I? I am strong and courageous, always ready for battle.

Who Am I? I am vigilant and have 20/20 vision in the Spirit.

Bibliography

Prince, D. *They Shall Expel Demons.* Grand Rapids, Mich.: Chosen Books, 1998.

Susan Y. Cambridge is a Licensed Clinical Social Worker in the State of Florida and a dedicated woman of the Lord who has been called, appointed, and anointed for this season. God has qualified her to help lead people through a process of deliverance, healing, and restoration, ultimately producing wholeness. Ms. Cambridge operates in a yoke-destroying anointing that has been birthed through intense prayer and adversity in her own life. She is a proud graduate of Fishers of Men Ministry Development Institute with an Ordination to the Gospel Ministry. She is also the founder of Miami's Chosen Generation, an agency whose ultimate goal is to provide foster care children an opportunity to be successful in life. Ms. Cambridge has expanded her enterprise as an author, motivational speaker, mentor, and entrepreneur. She is also a powerful intercessor who accurately hears the voice of the Lord and is willing to stand in proxy for others. Ms. Cambridge wholeheartedly believes that everyone has a newfound freedom awaiting them in Christ.